I0133156

STOIC FREEDOM

EPICTETUS' DISCOURES BOOK 4

STOICISM IN PLAIN ENGLISH

DR CHUCK CHAKRAPANI

THE STOIC GYM PUBLICATIONS

Copyright © 2018 by Chuck Chakrapani

All rights reserved. No part of this publication may be repro-
duced, distributed or transmitted in any form or by any means,
including photocopying, recording, or other electronic or me-
chanical methods, without the prior written permission of the
publisher, except in the case of brief quotations embodied in
critical reviews and certain other non-commercial uses per-
mitted by copyright law. For permission requests, write to the
publisher, addressed "Attention: Permissions Coordinator," at
the address below.

Stoic Gym Publications
www.thestoicgym.com

Ordering Information:
Quantity sales. Special discounts are available on quantity pur-
chases by corporations, associations, and others. For details,
contact the "Special Sales Department" at the address above.

Stoic Foundations/Chuck Chakrapani. —1st ed.
ISBNs:
Print: 978-0-920219-36-2
ePub: 978-0-920219-37-9
Mobi: 978-0-920219-38-6
PDF: 978-0-920219-39-3
18 19 20 21 22 23 24 25 26 27   1 2 3 4 5 6 7 8 9 0

Contents

Stoic Freedom

The Stoic goal is happiness. Not happiness in a narrow sense, but in a much more expansive sense. Stoic happiness or *eudemonia* is a way of thriving and flourishing. So, it is not just about being happy, but also about being tranquil, free, and fearless. The Stoic path to any one of these – happiness, tranquillity, or freedom – brings along with it the other aspects of flourishing as well.

Epictetus, perhaps because he spent the first two decades of his life as a slave, makes freedom his core focus. For Epictetus, freedom is synonymous with happiness. His discourses come back repeatedly to the theme of freedom. But what does it mean to be free? Epictetus explains:

You are free when you live as you wish; when you cannot be compelled, obstructed, or controlled; your choices cannot be blocked; when you get your desires fulfilled and when you don't face anything you want to avoid.

But is it possible to achieve this kind of freedom? What about the world we live in with so many constraints? Unscrupulous politicians, terrorists, violence, natural disasters, and insecurity surround us. Does it make sense even to think of the type of freedom that Epictetus talks about? Are his ideas outdated?

Epictetus might have lived 2,000 years ago, but the environment he lived in was far worse. He was born a slave and, until he was in his late teens, remained a slave. He lived under the rule of Nero. Roman emperors in those days were free to kill, imprison, or banish anyone and Nero was an extreme example of this. When Epictetus was set free, presumably after the death of Nero, he started to teach. Then he was banished by Emperor Domitian. Undeterred, he moved to the coastal city Nicopolis and continued to teach there. He was reputed to be lame as well. Yet Epictetus believed himself to be a free man. If the principles he taught made him free amid such adverse conditions, his advice is worth listening to.

Book IV of Epictetus' Discourses starts with a lengthy discourse on freedom, presumably the longest of all his discourses. The rest of the book keeps returning to the theme of freedom. Here is the summary of the basic themes.

Basic principles: A quick outline

1. *Your desires imprison you. If you confine your desire only to what is under your control, then you will never be unfree.* When we desire something that is not under our control, then anyone who has control over what we desire has power over us. When someone has

power over us, we cannot be free. But if you don't desire anything that is not under your control, then you cannot be compelled, obstructed, or controlled; your choices cannot be blocked; you get your desires fulfilled and you don't face anything you want to avoid. External things themselves are not the problem, but our hanging on to them is. You can still enjoy things that the world has to offer, if you are willing to let them go them at a moment's notice. When you align what you want to happen with what actually happens, you will be completely free. [1]

2. *Freedom has a price. If you want to be free, be prepared to pay.* Your freedom is a valuable thing. If you want it, you should give up something that is of equal value to you now. You may have to choose between being restrained and dignified over pointlessly wasting time over frivolous things. Make your choice. But no matter what you choose, do it whole-heartedly. If you try to do two things at once, you will achieve neither. [2, 3]

3. *The more value you attach to external things, the less free you are to choose.* Don't attach value to external things. Take them as they come. It is not what you do, but your judgments behind what you do that will decide whether you will be free or not. The more value you attach to any external thing – even if it a desirable thing – the less free you become. You become fearless when you stop valuing external things. [4, 7]

4. *A free person is not in conflict with anyone.* Pay attention to what you truly care about. Then you won't be

upset by what others think or say about you. When you don't value external things, other people's opinion and their behaviour becomes irrelevant to you. So, you cannot be upset by them or be in conflict with them. [5, 6]

5. *A free person is patient.* Free people are not carried away by external things, but take their time to judge things properly. They know that poor judgements are the cause of all evil and make sure they judge impressions correctly. They are patient and don't try to act before they are ready. [8]

6. *A free person is not envious.* When someone has things that you don't have, don't assume they got them for free. They paid a price in terms of flattering others, and putting up with things that they really didn't want to do. You, on the other hand, have your freedom. There is no need to envy others. [9]

7. *A free person is not anxious.* When you are anxious about the future, you want something that is not under your control. By being anxious about things you cannot control, you let go of things that are under your control. If you paid more attention to what is under your control and less attention to what is not, you would not be anxious. [10]

8. *A free person is pure.* A free person keeps themselves clean both in body and in mind. While they are cultivating their inner qualities, they won't neglect their outer appearance. [11]

9. *A free person is steadfast.* When you let your mind wander, it is not easy to bring it back. Therefore, you

should constantly keep the basic principles in mind and practice them. You don't need to be perfect. But if you let your mind wander or procrastinate, it will lead to more procrastination. [12]

10. *Free people choose what to reveal about themselves and when.* Free people are not quick to divulge personal information, just because someone else did so. They are not compelled to reciprocate confidences. They judge for themselves whether to divulge confidences.

CHAPTER 1

How to Achieve Freedom

Key ideas of this discourse

This is probably the longest of all Epictetus' discourses. Here he explores his central theme, human freedom.

1. *You are free when you live as you wish; when you cannot be compelled, obstructed, or controlled; your choices cannot be blocked; when you get your desires fulfilled, and when you don't face anything you want to avoid.*

2. *When you desire something, anyone who has power over that becomes your master.*

3. *To achieve freedom, eliminate your desires.*

4. *Understand fully what is under your control and what is not.*

5. *You can still enjoy things that the world has to offer, if you are willing to lose them any time without warning.*

6. *External things are not the problem, but our hanging on to them is.*

7. *We all have agreed-upon ideas. But we disagree on how those ideas apply in a given context.*

8. *When you align what you want to happen with what happens, you will be completely free.*

Who is free?

You are free when you live as you wish; when you cannot be compelled, obstructed, or controlled; your choices cannot be blocked; when you get your desires fulfilled, and when you don't face anything you want to avoid.

"Who wants to go through life, without knowing of how to achieve this?"

"No one."

"Who wants to be deceived, reckless, unjust, undisciplined, mean and ungrateful?"

"No one."

"So, no bad person lives the way they want. No bad person is free. Who wants to live in sorrow, fear, envy, and pity? Who wants to fail to get what they want and to get what they do not want?"

"No one."

"So, can we find a bad person free from fear, frustration, or misfortune?"

"No."

"So, we find no one who's free."

The many ways we are unfree

If you are a powerful person (such as a two-term consul), you will tolerate such talk only if I add, "But you are smart. This doesn't apply to *you*, of course." But if I tell you the truth and say, "You are as much a slave as one who is sold three times over," what can I expect but a punch in the nose?

"How can you call me a slave? My father is free, my mother is free, and there's no agreement for my selling me. Besides, I am a senator and a personal friend of the king himself. I have been twice consul and I have many working for me."

"Most worthy senator, in the first place, your father could have been a slave in the same sense that you are, along with your mother, your grandfather, and all your ancestors. And, even if they were all free, what does it prove? What if they were noble and you are mean-spirited? What if they were brave and you are a coward? And what if they were disciplined and you are unrestrained?

"What's that got to with being a slave?"

"Don't you see, when you act against your will under protest and compulsion, it is no different than being a slave?"

"Maybe. But who has the power to compel me except the king, who has power over everyone."

"So, you agree you have at least one master. Don't let the fact that he is also the master of others comfort you. It just means that you're a slave in a large household. You remind other citizens, 'Because of our master, we're free.'"

Let's set aside your master for a moment. Just tell me this.

"Have you ever been in love, maybe with a man or a woman, a free or an unfree person?"

"What that has to do with being free or being a slave?"

"Weren't you ever asked by the person you love to do something that you didn't want to do? Didn't you ever flatter her? Have you never kissed her feet? Yet, if someone forced you to kiss the feet of your master, you'd think it an outrage and the height of despotism. If this isn't slavery, then what is?"

Haven't you ever risked going out at night where you didn't want to go, spent more than you wanted, and said words of misery and woe, put up with being ridiculed and thrown out? If you are too embarrassed to admit it, observe the words and actions of [the mercenary soldier] Thrasonides who fought many campaigns, perhaps more than you. He went out at night even when [his slave] Geta wouldn't dare go. If he had been forced to go by his master, he would have gone out protesting loudly and complaining bitterly about his condition. What then does Thrasonides say? "No enemy could enslave me, and yet a pretty girl did." [From *Misoumenos* of Melander.] Poor guy, to be enslaved by a girl, a cheap one at that! How can you still call yourself free? What's the point in bragging about your military victories?

Then he asks for a sword to kill himself and gets angry at the person who, out of kindness, refuses to bring it. Then he sends gifts to his girl who despises him, and begs and weeps, and the moment he has had some success, he becomes ecstatic. But until he has learned to get rid of his lust and fear, how could he be free?

Think about how we apply the idea of freedom to animals. People raise lions in cages as tame animals, feed them, and even take them around with them. Who will say such an animal is free? Is it not true that the more softly a lion lives, the more slavish it is? And what lion that has sense and reason would care to be one of those lions? Birds, when they are caught and reared in cages, will do anything to escape. Some even prefer to starve themselves to death than endure such a life. Those that barely survive pine away and fly off the moment they get any opening. Such is their desire for natural freedom, to be independent and uncaged.

"Well, what's wrong with being here in a cage?"

"What a silly question! I was born to fly as I please, to live in the open air and sing. You want to take away all this from me and then ask, 'What's wrong with being here in a cage?'"

For this reason, we will call only those animals free that are not willing to be captive and, as soon as they are caught, escape by dying. It is for this reason [the Cynic philosopher] Diogenes says somewhere that one sure way to guarantee freedom is to be ready to die. He wrote to the King of Persia, "You can enslave the Athenians no more than you can enslave fishes."

"Why? Can't Athenians be captured?"

"Perhaps they can. But he moment they are captured, they will give you the slip and be gone, like a fish that dies when caught. If Athenians die like that when caught, what good is your military force?"

This is the voice of a truly free person who has deeply thought about freedom and found the truth about it. If you keep looking for it in the wrong place, is it any surprise that you won't find it?

Don't keep looking for freedom in the wrong places

A captive person wants to be set free. Why? Is it because he cannot wait to pay taxes when free? No, it is because he believes that, because he is not free he has been living in misery and with restrictions. He says,

"If I am set free, it's all happiness right away. I don't have to attend to anyone, I can talk to anyone on equal terms, I can come and go where I please."

Then he is set free. But he has nowhere to go and looks for someone to flatter to get his next meal. Then he sells his body, gets a sugar daddy, and finds himself in a far worse position than the one he escaped. Even if he makes a fortune, being a man of no taste, he falls for a cheap woman. In his misery he longs to be captive again and says,

"How was I any worse then? Someone fed me, clothed me, and took care of me when I was sick, while I did hardly anything in return. Now I have many masters instead of just one! But if I get a ring of office on my finger, then my life will be blissful and fulfilled."

To get them he suffers the humiliations that go with it. Then, when he gets them, it's the same old story all over again. Now he says,

"If I serve in the army, then all my troubles will be over."

So, he joins the army and goes off to a tour of duty and
suffers as much as any convict. He goes off on a second
tour of duty and then a third. Finally, he becomes a senator and finds himself a captive in fine and luxurious
company.

We fail to apply our preconceived ideas correctly to specific situations

Socrates used to say "Don't be foolish. Learn 'what every
specific thing means.'" [Xenophon's *Memorabilia*]. Don't
apply your preconceptions casually to things. You get
into trouble when you are unable to apply common preconceptions correctly to specific cases. Different people
think that different things are bad. Someone thinks she is
not well, but it is not true; the problem is she is not applying preconceived ideas correctly. Another imagines
he is poor, another thinks he has a harsh parent, and yet
another believes that powerful people don't care for her.
All these things really mean one thing and one thing only:
None of them knows how to apply their preconceived
ideas correctly.

After all, who does not have a preconceived idea of
what is bad? That it is harmful, we have to avoid it, and
we should use every means to get rid of it. Preconceived
ideas don't conflict among themselves. Conflict arises
when we start applying them.

What exactly is this bad and harmful thing that we
should get rid of? One person says that it is not being a
friend of Caesar. He's off the mark. He is not applying his

preconceived ideas right. He is upset and is seeking something that is not relevant. Even if he succeeds in getting the friendship he is after, he still hasn't got what he wants.

What he wants is what all of us want: To be peaceful and happy, to do what we like and not be forced to do what we don't like. But when he gets the friendship of Caesar, can he not be restrained or obstructed? Will he be happy and peaceful?

"Who will tell us this?"

Well, who better than this man here, already a friend of Caesar.

"So [friend of Caesar], please step up and tell us when did you sleep more soundly: now or before you became of friend Caesar?"

"Go away. Don't mock me. You have no idea how difficult it is for me. I barely start sleeping, a person comes in and announces, 'Caesar is up already and about to make and appearance.' Then come troubles and anxieties."

"So, when did you eat better, now or earlier?"

Listen to what he says here too: When he is not invited to dine with the emperor he is upset. When he is invited he dines like a slave dining with his master, anxious the whole time not to say or do anything stupid.

What do think he is afraid of? To be whipped like a slave? He should be so lucky. No, he is such a great man, a friend of Caesar and, as befits such men, his head might be chopped off. That's what he is afraid of.

"When were you more peaceful while taking a bath? When were you more relaxed while working out? In short, do you prefer: your present life or the previous one?"

"I bet that there's no one so stupid or forgetful that they don't regret being close to Caesar; the closer they are, the more they regret."

The person who controls what you desire controls you

If neither the so-called kings nor their friends live as they wish, who is left that can be called free? Look for it and you'll find nature has given you means for finding the truth. But if you find it difficult to find it by yourself, listen to those who looked for it before you. What do they say?

"Do you find freedom to be good?

"The best."

"Then, can someone who has obtained this greatest good be unhappy or unfortunate?"

"No."

"So, would you call someone who is unhappy, miserable, and mournful, unfree?"

"Yes."

"We now have gone beyond buying and selling stuff. Because, if you are right to agree with our discussion so far, then the Great King himself cannot be free if he is unhappy; neither can any prince, or consul, or two-term consul."

"Agreed."

"Now tell me this. Do you think that freedom is something grand, glorious, and valuable?"

"Why wouldn't I?"

"Is it possible that someone who has something this grand, glorious, and valuable be mean-spirited?"

"Impossible."

"Therefore, if you find someone grovelling before another, or flatter insincerely, without hesitation call them unfree. It doesn't matter if they do it to get a meal or a governorship, or a consulship. Call them petty slaves if they do it for petty rewards and call them slaves on a grand scale if they do it for big rewards."

"Again, I agree."

"Do you think that freedom is something independent and self-sufficient?"

"Yes, I do."

"Then anyone who can be hindered and compelled by someone else is not free. Don't be concerned about the status of their ancestors, or whether he was ever bought or sold. If someone calls another 'Master' with feeling call him a slave, even if twelve attendants go ahead of him. Or, if you hear, 'God, the things I have to put up with!', call that person a slave. In short if you find anyone moaning, complaining, or miserable, call him a slave in a purple toga."

"What if he doesn't do any of these things?"

"Still, don't call him free yet. Find out how he judges. See if he feels boxed in, disappointed, or dissatisfied. If you find any of these, call him a slave on holiday at

Saturnalia [where slaves had special privileges]. Say that his master is away. He will soon return, and you will see his true condition."

"When who returns?"

"Whoever has the power to give or take away the things he values."

"Do we have many masters, then?"

"We do. Even when there is no one else, circumstances are our masters – and there are many. Anyone who controls any one of them controls us all."

Understand clearly what you control and what you don't

After all, no one fears Caesar himself. What one really fears is death, deportation, loss of property, jail and loss of civil rights. Neither does anyone love Caesar, unless he is personally deserving. What one loves is money or the high office. When we love, or loathe, or fear these things, anyone who controls them becomes our master. This is inevitable. That's why we treat them like gods. If they have the power over most benefits we seek, then we treat them as divine. Then we think of the false minor premise, "*This* person has the power to benefit me the most," which inevitably leads to false conclusions.

"What then makes a person free and be his own master?"

"Because money, status, and even a kingdom are not the answer, we must find something else. Tell me, how does a person write freely and fluently?"

"By knowing how to write well."

"How does a person play the harp well?"

"By knowing how to play the harp."

"Therefore, it follows that in life also we need to know how to live well. You have heard this as a general principle but now think how it applies to specific cases. Suppose what you want is under the control of someone else. Is it possible for you, then, to be free and unrestricted?"

"No."

"So, you cannot be free. Now consider this. What is under your control: everything, nothing, or some things?"

"What do you mean?"

"Is it under your control that your body *always* performs perfectly?"

"No."

"Is it healthy whenever you wish?

"No."

"To live or die?"

"No."

"So, the body isn't yours. It can be controlled by what is stronger than itself."

"Quite so."

"What about land? Can you have as much as you want, as long as you want, in the way you want?"

"No"

"People who work for you?"

"No."

"Your clothes?"

"No."

"Your house?"

"No."

"Your pet animals?"

"No. None of this is."

"Well, if you want so much for your children, your wife, your brother, or your friends to live. Is this under your control?"

"No, not this either."

"Is there nothing at all that is within your total power and control?"

"I don't know."

"Well, look at this way. Can anyone make you agree to something that is not true?"

"No, no one can."

"So, in the area of assent, no one can force or obstruct you."

"That's for sure."

"Can anyone make you choose something that you really don't want?"

"Yes. They can threaten me with death or punishment and force me to do things."

"What if you don't care about dying or being punished? Can they still force you?"

"No."

"What do you think about death? Is your attitude to death under your control?"

"It is."

"Is directing your impulses your own action or not?"

"I have to admit it is."

"And the choice to do something – that is under your control as well."

"Yes, but what if I choose to walk and someone stands in my way?"

"What part can they obstruct? Not your decision?"

"No, but my poor body."

"Yes. A rock might obstruct it as well."

"So be it. Still I can't go for my walk."

"Who told you that walking is under your total control and no one can stop you? What I said was your choice cannot be obstructed. But when it comes to using your body and whether it co-operates are not, I have told you long ago, nothing is your own."

"I will agree to that as well."

"Can anyone force you to desire something you do not want?"

"No one."

"Or propose or plan something or deal with your impressions in any way?"

"No, they cannot. But if I desire something, they can stop me from getting what I want."

"If you desire something under your control, how can they stop you?"

"They can't."

"And who said that, when you desire what is not your control, you can't be stopped?"

"Are you saying, then, I can't desire health?"

"No. Nor anything else that is not under your control."

If you cannot get or keep something at will, then it is not your own. Keep your hands, and more importantly your desire, far away from it. Otherwise, you will be making yourself a slave, putting your head under the yoke. The same thing happens if you value something that is not under your control; or develop a passion for something under someone else's control, or that is perishable.

"Isn't my hand my own?"

"It's a part of you. But by nature, it is dirt, subject to restraint and force and therefore a slave to anything physically stronger."

Be prepared to let go of things that are not your own

And why pick on your hand? As long as it lasts, the whole body should be thought of as a loaded donkey. If a soldier demands it for public service and takes it away, let it go. Don't resist or grumble; you'll be beaten, and you'll lose the donkey anyway. If this is how you should treat your body, how should you treat things that serve the body? If your body is a donkey, then you have a donkey's bridle, pack-saddles, shoes, barley, and fodder. Let them go too. Give them up even more quickly and more cheerfully than you did the donkey.

"When you are so prepared and trained to distinguish what is your own from what it not;

to know what can be obstructed from what cannot; and

to see clearly that what cannot be obstructed is your only concern, is there anyone to be afraid of anymore?"

"No."

"Of course not. What is there for you to be afraid about? About things that are your own in which good and evil reside? Who has the power over these? Who can take them away? Who can block them? No one can anymore they can hinder God. Or is it your body and property – things that are not your own and of no value to you – that you are afraid for? What else have you been studying from the beginning except distinguishing between what is your own and what it is not, what is in your power and what is not, what can be blocked and what cannot? What's your purpose in talking to philosophers? So, you could be as lost and miserable as before; not be free of fear and anxiety?"

What has pain to do with you? Only when you anticipate something fearful and it becomes true, is it painful.

What will you desire now? All your desires are now only for things under your control as they are good and within reach. You want nothing outside your sphere of choice. So, there is no place for irrational or impulsive desire.

When this is your attitude, who can intimidate you? How can one person be intimidated by another – by appearance, speech, or meeting? It is no more possible than that a horse, a dog, or a bee can make another horse, dog, or bee intimidated. No. What makes people afraid is things? Whenever someone has the power to give or take away things from you, you become fearful.

External things are not the problem, our judgments about them are

[The dialogue that follows is based on a complicated metaphor of tyrants, fortress and bodyguards. It is explained along these lines by W.A. Oldfather: The fortress and the bodyguards are actual external things such as wealth and reputation, which are harmless in themselves. They become dangerous only when you judge them falsely to be of value. The tyrants are our false judgments which make us believe that external things are of value. Once we get rid of our false judgments, there's no need to get rid of the external things themselves. They may hurt those who hold false judgments about them, but not us. We cannot get rid of all external things anyway. Some, like death and disease, are inevitable. Therefore, every person must do the work for themselves and get rid of false judgments. The main point of this metaphor is that you can't be free just by getting rid of external things, because they're harmless. You can only be free by getting rid of your false judgments about them.]

"How to destroy the tyrant's fortress?"

"Not by weapons or by fire but by judgements. But if we destroy the fortress, do we also destroy our judgements about fever, and about pretty women? Do we destroy the things in our internal fortress, along with the inner tyrants who torture us every day, though they may look different at different times?

"No."

"It is here you must begin. You must attack the fortress and drive out the tyrants. Give up your body and its different parts, your influence, property, reputations, offices, honours, children, brothers, and your friends. They're not your own. When the tyrants are driven out there's no need to destroy the fortress, as far as I am concerned. It does no harm to anyone by being there. You don't have to drive out the bodyguards. They can stay. How can they affect you? Their sticks, spears, and knives are meant for others, not for you."

Align your wants to conform to reality

Personally speaking, I was never kept from something I wanted or forced to have something I did not want. How did I manage it? By subjecting my will to God.

- Does He want me to be sick? So do I.
- Does He want me to choose something? So do I.
- Does He want me to want something? So do I.
- Does He want me to get something? So do I.
- Does He not want me to get it? Neither do I.

So, I say yes even to death and torture. Who can stop me now? Who can force on me what I do not want? I'm as completely free from hindrance and compulsion as God himself.

[Another way to interpret the above is to say that when we don't fight or complain about the inevitable realities of our life – where we don't have a choice anyway – and act only on things that are in our control, we become unstoppable. As psychologist and philosopher

William James put it, "Be willing to have it so. Acceptance of what has happened is the first step to overcoming the consequences of any misfortune."]

This is how cautious travellers act as well. When they hear that there are robbers along the way, they do not go off on their own but wait for a group of people who travel together and go with them. A sensible person will behave the same way in life, thinking, "There are many thieves and bandits, many storms and many chances to lose my valuable things. How can I be safe? How can I escape thieves and robbers? Who should I attach myself to? Some rich and powerful person? What good will it do me if he loses his position and breaks down? What if my travel companion himself turns against me and robs me? What should I do?" By thinking this way, the traveller concludes that if he allied himself with God he would safely complete his journey.

"What do you mean by 'allied himself'?"

"It means acting in such a way that whatever God wants, that is what we also want. If he doesn't want something, we don't want it either."

"How can we do this?"

"By paying attention to his purpose and design."

Enjoy what is given to you, for the time it is given to you

What has he given me as my own and what has he kept for himself? He has given me power over my choices, free of all restrictions and compulsions. How can he make the body, which is made of dirt, unrestricted? So, he put it along with other things in the cosmic cycle such as my property, my furniture, my house, my children, and my spouse. Why should I fight against it? Why should I try to grab something that lies outside the area of my choice, something that doesn't belong to me? [While they are given to me] I'll keep them in the spirit they are given, for as long as possible. One who has given it can also take it away. Why should I resist? It would foolish to resist someone who's stronger than me. More than that, it would be wrong.

Where did I get things when I came into this world? My father gave them to me. Who gave them to him? And who made the Sun, the fruits, the seasons, human fellowship and social order?

You have received everything – including your life – from your benefactor. Yet, you are angry with the giver for taking things back?

Who are you? Why did you come here? Isn't it God who brought you here? Hasn't he shown you the light? Hasn't he given you the people who support you? Hasn't he given you your senses? Hasn't he given you reason?

How did he bring you here? As a mortal, as one who would live here in flesh for a while, witness his grand design, and share briefly the pageant and the festival with him. So why not enjoy the feast and pageant while you are able? And when the time is up and when he leads you out, why not go out thanking him for what you have seen and heard?

"But I want to enjoy the festival a while longer."

"Yes. So would newcomers to mysteries – they would like the initiation ceremonies to continue. So would the Olympic crowd – they would like to see more contestants. But the festival is over. Discreetly move on. Be grateful for what you have seen."

Make room for others to get in. It is now their time to be born, as it was yours once. And, when they are born, they need a place to live. Their necessities of life need to be taken care of. But if those who came earlier wouldn't leave, what would happen? Why are you so greedy and dissatisfied? Why do you crowd the world?

"Yes, but I want my wife and children with me."

"Why? Are they yours? Don't they belong to the one who gave them to you? The one who created you as well? Will you hang on to what's not yours and refuse to give them up? Do you want to challenge someone better?"

"Why did he bring me in this world with all these conditions attached?"

"If you don't like it, leave. He doesn't need fault finders. He needs those who are keen to join in the festival and the dance – those who would applaud the festival with their praise and acclaim. He wouldn't mind dismissing the grumpy and the cowardly."

How to use external things

Even when such people are invited, they don't act as though they are at a festival or play their proper role. Instead they whine, find fault with God, their fortune, and their fellow human beings. They don't appreciate their

own powers and resources given to them for the opposite purpose – to be generous, high-minded, courageous,
and free – exactly what we are talking about now.

"Then why did I get the external things?"

"To use them."

"For how long?"

"For as long as the lender pleases."

"What if I can't live without them?"

"They won't be, if you don't get attached to them.
Don't tell yourself that they are essential, and they
aren't."

This is what you should practice from dawn to dusk.
Begin with the least valuable and fragile thing like a jug
or a cup. Then apply the same idea to clothes, pets, and
property. Finally, apply the idea to yourself, your body
parts, your children, your wife and others. Look around
you in every direction. Mentally get rid of everything.
Keep your judgments pure. See that you are attached to
nothing that doesn't belong to you and can be painful if
taken away from you. While you are training yourself
every day, don't be pretentious and say that you are "pur-
suing philosophy." Rather say that you are preparing for
your liberation.

True freedom

For this is true freedom. This is the freedom that Antisthenes gave Diogenes who said that never again would
he be a slave to anyone. Then he was captured by the pi-
rates. What did he do? Did he call any of them his

'master'? Did he use any other word that would mean the same thing? No. He screamed at them for feeding their prisoners badly. How did he behave when he was sold? He immediately started criticizing his new master – that he shouldn't dress this way, or shave that way, and that he should teach his sons to live differently. Why not? If the same master had bought a personal trainer, he would have used the trainer as his master as far as exercises are concerned. The same goes if the master had bought a doctor or architect. In every field, the person with skill is superior to one without. So, in general, how can a person with knowledge of how to live be anything but the master?

"Who is the master of the ship?"

"The captain."

"Why? Because if you disobey him you will be punished."

"But so-and-so can also punish me."

"But not without consequences."

"I thought he could."

"If he punishes without having the authority to do so, he cannot get away with it."

"How would a master who puts me in chains be punished?"

"The very act puts *him* in chains. You yourself know this is true if you accept that human beings are civilized animals and not wild beasts. Answer this: When does a plant do badly?"

"When it goes against its nature."

"When does a bird do badly?"

"When it goes against its nature."

"So it is with humans. What then is human nature? Biting, kicking, throwing someone in prison or killing him? No, but being kind, cooperative, and having good will toward others. Like it or not, he feels badly whenever he acts unreasonably."

"So, Socrates didn't do poorly then?"

"No, but his jurors and accusers did."

"How about Helvidius at Rome?"

"He didn't. But his murderer did."

"How do you figure that?"

"You don't say that a cock that just won has fared badly, even if severely wounded; but rather the one that is beaten without a scratch. You don't call a dog happy if he doesn't hunt or work, but only when you see him sweating, labouring and exhausted by the chase. What is odd in saying evil is everything that's contrary to nature? Don't you say this about other things? Why do you make human beings the only exception?

"When we say that human beings by nature are gentle, affectionate, and faithful, aren't we being ridiculous?"

"No, we are not."

"Isn't it the reason why people don't suffer even when they are beaten, jailed, or killed? And the victim may be dignified in his suffering and come through as a better and more advantaged person? Isn't it also true that the person who is really harmed, suffers the most, and is disgraced, is the one who has become a wolf, a snake, or a wasp instead of a human being?"

A Summary of the principles

Very well then. Let's review what we agreed on.

- The person who is not blocked and has ready at hand whatever he needs is free.
- The person who can be blocked or forced to do against their will is a slave.
- You cannot be blocked if you don't desire external things, things that are not your own.
- What things are not your own? Things over which you don't have the power to decide – to have or not to have, to have in the way you want, or at the time you want. Our body, its different parts, and our property, therefore, are not our own.

This is the road that leads to freedom. This is the only road that frees you from slavery. This is what make you say at any time from the bottom of your heart

Lead me Zeus, Lead me, Destiny
To the goal I was long assigned.

A challenge to the student

"What do you say, Philosopher? A powerful person calls you and asks you bear false witness. Do you go along with it or not?"

"Let me think it over."

"You're going to think it over now? Weren't you thinking over it when you were in school? Didn't you learn what things are good, what things are bad, and what things are indifferent?"

"I did."

"And?"

"The right and noble actions are good; wrong and shameful actions are bad."

"Is living good?"

"No."

"Is dying bad?"

"No."

"And prison?"

"No."

"And what about slanderous and dishonest talk, betraying of a friend, or the flattering of an oppressor? How do they strike you?

"As bad."

Clearly, you are not thinking through this. You haven't done so in the past either. Really, how much do you need to think it over – to decide that you should exercise your power to get the greatest goods and avoid the greatest evils? A fine subject for thinking – requires a lot of thought indeed! Who are you trying to fool? You never thought this through. If you had really understood that vice alone is bad and everything else is indifferent, you wouldn't need time to "think it over." You would have been able to decide right away using your reason as readily as you use your vision. Do you have to think it over whether black is white? Or, whether light is heavy? No, these things follow from the clear evidence of your senses.

Why then are you now "thinking it over" whether indifferents are more to be avoided than evils? These are not your judgments, are they? You don't think that jail and death are indifferents, do you? Rather, you think they are the greatest evils.

This is the habit you have been developing from the beginning.

"Where were you?"

"I was in the classroom."

"Who were you listening to?"

"I was talking with philosophers. Now I have left school, I don't care for those finicky and foolish teachers."

This is how a friend is condemned by a philosopher. This is how he becomes a parasite, this is how he sells himself for money, and this is how he betrays his beliefs when meeting with the Senators. Inside him, though, his true judgments are loudly crying out. These are not some half-hearted thoughts that he is barely hanging onto as a result of empty discussions. These are his true convictions derived from his initiation and training. [According to William Oldfather, the above probably refers an incident that happened during Nero's reign when Epictetus was still a boy in which Egnatius Celer accused his friend, Barea Soranus.]

"Watch yourself carefully and see how you take the news. I don't say your child has died, because you may not be able to endure it. I say your oil is spilled or someone drank up all your wine."

"What if someone says, 'Hey philosopher, you talked differently when you were in school. Who are you trying to fool? Why call yourself a human being when you're a worm?'"

"I'd like to know how much self-control *they* have when they're having sex. I'd like to see how they control themselves and hear the sounds they make. Whether they even remember their name or any of the discourses they had heard or taught."

"What has this got to do with freedom?"

"This has everything to do with freedom, whether you rich people like it or not."

"And your proof is...?"

As long as you have a master, you're a slave

"What else, but you yourselves. You have this master [the emperor] and you live at his beck and call. You faint when he just looks at you with a scowl on his face. You say before the old men and women of the court, "I can't possibly do this. I am not allowed." Why aren't you allowed? Weren't you just telling me that you were free?"

"But Aprulla [a rich old woman] won't let me."

"Tell the truth then, slave. Don't run away from your masters, don't deny having them, and don't say that you are free when there is so much proof that you are just a slave. If someone who is desperately in love does something against their better judgement, one can at least pity them because they are in the grip of an uncontrollable passion and in a manner of speaking, divine. But who can put up with you – you have a passion for old men and old women, you wipe their noses, wash them, bribe them with your gifts, wait upon them when they are sick; yet, at the same time, you are praying for their death and asking the doctors if they are about to die. Or when you kiss the hands of other people's slaves for the sake of high honours and offices you make yourself a slave of slaves. What can you expect then?"

And then you proudly wander around as a magistrate or a consul. Do you think I don't know who gave you that position and how you got it? If I were you, I would rather die than owe my life to Felicio [a freed slave of Nero], putting up with his rudeness and arrogance. I know how a slave behaves when he gets influence and importance.

"Are *you* free then?"

"God, I wish and pray to be. But I still can't face my masters. I continue to value my body and try to keep it healthy, although it is hardly healthy. But if you want to see an example, I will point to Diogenes."

Examples of free people:
Diogenes and Socrates

Diogenes was free. Why? Not because his parents were free because they weren't. He was free himself because he got rid of all handles of slavery. There was no way anyone could get close to him, capture him, and make him a slave. Everything he owned was only loosely tied to him. He could let go of everything. If you grabbed his property, he would rather let you have it than be pulled along with it. If you grabbed his leg, he would let go of his leg; if you grabbed hold his body, he would let go of his body. The same with family, friends, and country [the universe itself]. He was aware where they all came from, who gave them, and the conditions attached to them.

But he would never have given up his true parents [the gods] and his real country. He was more obedient to gods than anyone else. He was more willing to die for his country than anyone else. He didn't pretend to care for the world for show. He was constantly aware that everything that comes into being has a source. Things happen for the sake of the universe at the command of its governor.

So, pay attention to what he says and writes.

"Diogenes, here is why you can speak your mind to the Persian king, and the Spartan king Archedamus."

Was it because his parents were free? No. No Athenian, Corinthian, or Spartan could speak to the kings as they pleased, but feared and flattered instead, because all their parents were slaves. Someone asked him:

"Why are you then allowed to speak the way you like?"

"Because I don't consider my body my own. Because I need nothing, and law is everything to me. I don't care for anything else."

That's what made him free.

Just in case you think I chose an easy example of a person without family and social responsibilities (as a solitary person has fewer demands on him to bend the rules), consider Socrates. He had both a wife and children, but he treated them as though they were on loan. He had a country which he served as far as it was duty and for as long as it was his duty. He had friends and relatives, but he treated them as less important than the law and the need to obey it.

When he was drafted, he was the first one to leave home. He faced danger without flinching. When the Thirty Tyrants ordered him to arrest Leon [a leader of the opposition, who they wanted to murder], he never bothered to do anything about it, because he thought it was unlawful. Yet he knew he might die if he refused. But he didn't care. He was not trying to save his life but his integrity and his honour. These are not matters up for negotiation.

Then, when he was on trial for his life, did he behave like someone with a wife and children? No. He behaved like someone who is not attached. How did he behave when it was time to drink the poison? Crito urged him to escape for the sake of his children, what did he answer? Did he think that this was a stroke of luck? No way. He thought about the right course of action and nothing else. He said that he didn't want to save his body but the element that grew and thrived by justice but diminished and was destroyed by injustice. He didn't save his life by acting shamefully. Socrates, who resisted the Athenians' demand to vote on an illegal motion, who defied the Thirty Tyrants, who spoke so eloquently about excellence and goodness – such a man is not saved by any shameful means. He is saved by dying and not by running away.

He was like a good actor who leaves the stage as soon as his role comes to an end.

"What will happen to your children?"

"If I had gone off to another city, you would have taken care of them. If I go off this world, would no one take care of them?"

See how he treats death lightly and jokes about it. If it had been you or I, we would have used philosophical principles to prove that those who act unjustly should be paid back in kind. And then add, "If I escape, I can help many people. If I die, I will be able to help no one." If there was a mouse-hole of an opening, we would have squeezed through.

But how could we possibly be of use to anyone, with all our friends left behind? Or, if we were useful when alive, wouldn't we be even more useful to the world by dying at the right time, in the right way? Now that Socrates is dead, his memory is even more useful to us than what he said and did while he was alive.

If you want to be free, if you understand the true value of your goal, then study these principles, these judgments, these arguments, and think about these examples. Does it come as a surprise to you that such a great goal needs many sacrifices? What people commonly consider as freedom, many had hanged themselves, thrown themselves over cliffs. Occasionally, even entire cities have been destroyed. So, for the sake of the true, secure, and unshakable freedom, will you not return to God what he gave you when he asks for it? As Plato says, be prepared not only to die but to be tortured, deported, beaten – in short, to give back everything that is not your own. Otherwise, you will be a slave among slaves – even if you are a consul a thousand times over, and even if you go up to the Palace – you will remain a slave all the same.

And you will see what Cleanthes meant when he said that, "Perhaps philosophers do things that are contrary to expectation, but not contrary to reason." You will find this to be true. The things that are eagerly sought after and admired are of no use to you once you get them. Meanwhile, those who don't have them imagine that everything good will be theirs once they get these things. And then they get them. Yet their longing and anxiety remain unchanged. So is their desire for what they don't have.

Freedom is not achieved by fulfilling your desires, but by eliminating them

You cannot achieve freedom by fulfilling your desires, but only by eliminating them. To fully understand how true this is, work on these principles as diligently as you worked on your other things. Stay up late into the night to develop a liberated frame of mind. Cultivate the company of a philosopher instead of a rich old man. Hang around at the philosopher's door. There's no shame in it and you will not come back empty-handed or without profit, if you go there with the right attitude. At least try it. There is no shame in it.

Think about this

Free is the person who lives as he wishes and cannot be coerced, impeded or compelled, whose impulses cannot be thwarted, who always gets what he desires and never has to experience what he would rather avoid. Discourses IV.1.1.

Epictetus [RD]

CHAPTER 2

Be Committed to Your Choice

Key ideas of this discourse

1. *Everything comes at a price.*
2. *You can choose either restraint and dignity or having a good time without regard to anything else.*
3. *You can have either, but you have to choose one.*
4. *No matter what you choose, do it whole-heartedly.*

Everything comes at a price

You should take care of this first before you do anything else: Be careful when associating with your former friends and acquaintances so you don't sink to their level. Otherwise you may ruin yourself. You may be bothered by the idea that they might think you are awkward and so treat you differently. But remember; everything comes at a price. You can't act the same way as you did before and yet be different.

Be single-minded about being a better person

So, choose. Do you want to go back to your old ways, so you may have the love of your friends, or be a better person even if you lose their affection? If you choose to be a better person, stick to it from now on. Let nothing distract you from this goal. You cannot make progress if you waver. If you are committed to this and ready to put in the effort, then give up everything else. Otherwise, by trying to be both at the same time, you will pay a double penalty. You will neither make progress nor retain the earlier friendships.

Before now, when you spent all your time doing frivolous things, your friends found you very agreeable. But you can't do both equally well. If you follow one course of action, the other will fall short. If you don't go out drinking with your old buddies the same way you did before, they won't be too pleased with you.

So, choose. Do you want to be a charming drunk in their company or boring and sober on your own? If you don't sing with them, you won't please them as much as you did before.

So, again, choose.

No matter what you choose, do so whole-heartedly

If you value restraint and dignity over your old friends saying, "What a great guy!" then forget all other things, give them up, and walk away. Have nothing more to do with them. If you don't like that, then commit to the other choice whole-heartedly. Be one of those degenerates, one of those adulterers, and indulge in your every impulse and desire to get what you want. Jump up in the theatre. Loudly applaud the dancer.

What you cannot do is to mix the two roles. You cannot be both Thersites *and* Agamemnon. Thersites was crippled and bald. Agamemnon was tall and handsome and loved his people.

Think about this

[Remember] everything comes at a price. It isn't possible to change your behaviour and still be the same person as before. Discourses IV.2.2 Epictetus [RD]

CHAPTER 3

Guard Your Freedom

Key ideas of this discourse

1. When you lose an external thing, you get something in return. Think about what you get in return when you lose an external thing.
2. Your freedom is a valuable thing. You will not get anything of equal value for giving it up.
3. Therefore, be awake and be on guard for your freedom.

Think about what you get in return when you lose an external thing

You should always think this when you lose any external thing: What did you get in return? If it was of greater value, don't you say you lost anything. It may be a horse for a donkey, an ox for a sheep, a good action for a small sum of money, peace for foolish chatter, or self-respect for indecent talk. If you remember this, you will always maintain your character. If you don't, you are wasting your time. All your current undertakings and efforts will come to nothing.

Not much is needed to destroy and upset everything – just a slight deviation from reason will do. A captain needs less skill to overturn a ship than to keep it safe. If he turns it a little too far into the wind, he is lost. Even if he doesn't do it deliberately, but briefly loses his concentration for a moment, he is lost.

You are guarding your freedom, which is no small thing

It is so in life as well. Even if you nod off briefly, you could lose all that you have learned. So, pay attention to your sense impressions. Be awake and watch over them. It is no small thing that you are guarding – you are guarding self-respect, fidelity, constancy, a tranquil mind undisturbed by fear, pain, or confusion – in a word, freedom. What will you sell all these for? Look, how valuable are they?

"I cannot get anything of that much value in return."

Yes. I have modest behaviour; he has a high office. I have self-respect; he has the office of the magistrate. I don't shout when it is not called for. I don't stand up when I should not. For I am a free man, a friend of God. I obey him of my own free will. But I should not lay claim to anything else – body, property, office, reputation – nothing, in short. God doesn't want me to claim these things either. If it was his desire, he would have made them good for me. He hasn't done so and I won't disobey his orders.

In everything you do, guard your own good

In everything you do, guard your own good. As for the rest, be happy to take things as they come and use them rationally. Otherwise you will have bad luck and no good luck, and you will be restrained and blocked. These are the laws that have been sent to you from above. These are the laws that you should interpret and obey and not the laws of Masurius and Cassius [the two distinguished jurists at that time.]

Think about this

Guard your good in everything you do; and for the rest be content to take simply what has been given you. Discourses IV.3.11. Epictetus [WO]

CHAPTER 4

Act on What You Learned

Key ideas of this discourse

1. *Any desire – be it for money or for peace – makes you a slave.*

2. *Read with a view to act on what you learn.*

3. *The more value you attach to external things, the less free you are to choose.*

4. *Always remember what is under your control and what is not.*

5. *When you desire or feel averse to something, you become a slave to the one who controls the object of your desire and aversion.*

6. *Take things as they come.*

7. *It is not your action, but your judgement that gave rise to the action, that decides whether it is good or bad.*

Any desire, even a desire for peace, can make you a slave

A desire for money and power makes you miserable and submissive to others. But so does its opposite, a desire for leisure, peace, travel, and learning. As a rule, if we attach value to externals of any kind, it would make us submissive to others. It makes little difference whether you *want* to be a senator or *not want* to be one; whether you *want* to hold office or *not* want to hold office; whether you say, "I'm in a bad way. I can't do anything because I am tied to books," or you say, "I'm in a bad way. I've no time to read." A book is external. So is a position external, like honour and office.

Why do you want to read anyway? For entertainment or to learn something? Either way, you are being frivolous and lazy. Judged by proper standards, reading should lead you to peace. If it doesn't, what good is it?

"But reading does make me peaceful. That's exactly why I am unhappy when I'm deprived of it."

"What kind of peace is this if it can be so easily disturbed? Not even by the Emperor or a friend of the Emperor but by a crow, a flute player, fever, or thirty thousand other things? True peace of mind is continuous and undisturbed."

Now I am asked to do something. I'll do it. I will pay attention to the boundaries that I need to respect; act confidently but also with restraint; and without desire or aversion regarding externals. At the same time, I pay attention to other people's words and actions. I don't do this looking for an opportunity to criticize or ridicule them but to make sure that I don't make the same mistakes.

"How do I do stop it, then?"

"I used to make the same mistake once. But, thank God, not anymore."

If you have acted thus and made it your concern, isn't it as good as having read or written a thousand lines? When you eat, do you wish you were reading? Aren't you happy to be eating in a manner you learned by reading? The same goes for bathing and exercising. Why don't you behave the same way whether you meet a powerful person or an ordinary person? If you are calm, poised and dignified, if you observe what is happening (rather than being observed) around you, if you don't envy those who are honoured ahead of you, and if you don't let externals confuse you, what else do you need? Books? Why? For what purpose?

"Isn't reading a kind of preparation for living?"

"But there is more to life than reading. It is like an athlete entering a stadium and immediately complaining that he is not in the gym working out."

This was why you did your workouts, trained with weights, practiced in the ring with your sparring partners. Are you looking for these now when it is time to act? It is as if, when it is time to deal with impressions and judge them to be true or not, you are looking to read the book *On Comprehension*! Why is this? It's because you never read for this purpose; you never wrote for this purpose – the purpose of using the impressions we receive in accordance with nature. Instead, what you care about is to learn what was written on the subject, so you can explain it to someone else; how to analyse an argument or examine the hypothetical argument.

Read not just to know, but to act on what you read

Where you are enthusiastic about something, there you are bound to face obstacles. You desire what is not under your control? Be prepared to be obstructed, to be frustrated, and to fail. But,

- if you read *On Choice* not out of idle curiosity but to choose the right course of action;
- if you read *On Desire and Aversion* so you may never fail to get what you want and not get what you don't want; and
- if you read *On Duty* so in your social relationships you never do anything irrational or inappropriate;

then we wouldn't be frustrated or become impatient with our reading. We would be happy to act on what we have learned. Instead of saying, "I have written so many pages today; I have read so many pages today," you will say, "Today I made choices in the way that the philosophers teach; I stayed away from desires, and was averse only to things under my control; I wasn't flustered by so-and-so or angered by so-and-so. I was patient, restrained, and co-operative." This is the way to thank God for what we should be thankful for.

As it is, we don't recognize how similar we are to the crowd in other ways as well. Others are afraid that they won't hold office while you are afraid that you will. Don't be concerned. Just as you laugh at others, laugh at yourself too. What is the difference between a person with fever who craves water and a person with rabies who is afraid of water? How can you be like Socrates who said, 'If it pleases the gods, so be it"?

Do you think that, if Socrates had decided to linger in the Lyceum or the Academy talking to the young people there, he would have served so readily in so many campaigns? No. He would have moaned and groaned, "Poor me! Here I am feeling miserable. I could have been back at the Lyceum, enjoying the sun.

Is that your job. Sunning yourself? Is it not to be happy? Is it not to be free of obstructions and restraints? How would he have been still Socrates if he had groaned and moaned? How would have gone on to write hymns of praise in prison?

Don't complain

Remember this. The more value you attach to external things, the less free you are to choose. Things outside our control include not only office but freedom from office also; not only business but leisure also.

"Should I then spend my life in this chaos among the mob?"

"What do you mean by chaos? Among the mob? What's hard about that? Imagine you are at the Olympics.

Regard the chaos as a festival. There too, one man shouts this, another man that. One pushes the other. Even in swimming pools there are many people. Yet, who doesn't enjoy the Olympics and feel sorry to leave?

Don't be hard to please. Don't complain about trivial things. "The vinegar is bad, it's sharp; the honey is foul, it upsets my stomach; I don't like the vegetables. Similarly, people say, "I don't like leisure, it's lonely; I don't like a crowd, it is noisy." If you happen to find yourself alone or with a few other people, call this peace and go along for the duration. Talk to yourself, work on your impressions, and sharpen your preconceptions. But, if you happen to find yourself in a crowd, call it the games, a festival, or a celebration. Try to share the festival with the world. After all, what is more pleasing to a lover of human kind than the sight of many people? We take pleasure in seeing herds of cows and horses. We take delight in watching a fleet of ships. Why, then, hate the sight of a group of humans?

"But they are loud. I'll go deaf."

"All right. You go deaf. What's it to you? Will it stop you from judging impressions correctly? Who can stop you from using desire and aversion, choice and refusal according to nature? No noise, no shouting is loud enough to do that."

Remember these central questions

Remember these central questions:

- What is yours?

- What is not yours?
- What is given to you?
- What does God say that you should do now?
- What does God say that you should not do?

A little while ago, God wanted you to take some time off, communicate with yourself, write, read, and hear about these things and prepare yourself. You had the time available for it. Now he is saying, "Come. Now take the test. Show us what you have learned and how well you have trained. How long do you plan on working out alone? It is time for you to find out whether you are an athlete who deserves to win or one of those who travel around the world, only to be defeated everywhere."

If you want peace, don't be a slave to desires

Why, then, are you upset? No public contest is without commotion. There must be trainers, supporters who cheer, many official supervisors, and many spectators.

"But I want to live in peace."

"Well then, mope and be miserable. That is what you deserve. What greater punishment do you deserve for ignoring and challenging God's will than to be miserable, dissatisfied and envious? Don't you want to free yourself from all this?"

"Yes, but how can I do that?"

"You have heard often that you must get rid of your desires completely and be averse only to things that are within your power. You must give up all external things – body, reputation, fame, books, applause, office, and freedom from office. Because desiring any of these things immediately makes you a slave, you are a subject, you can be restrained and compelled, and you are entirely at the control of others. Keep this verse by Cleanthes handy:

"Lead me, Zeus; lead me, Destiny"

Take things as they come

Do I have to go to Rome? I go to Rome. To Gyara? I go to Gyara. To Athens? I go to Athens. To prison? I go to prison. But if you say, "When do we get to Athens?" you are lost. If you don't get to Athens, you will be disappointed because your desire is not fulfilled. If you do get to Athens, you will be overjoyed for the wrong reasons. Again, if you are stopped from getting what you want, you are stuck with what you don't want. Therefore, forget these things.

"But Athens is beautiful."

"But happiness is much more beautiful; and having a peaceful and undisturbed mind, dependent on only yourself."

"But Rome is so crowded and noisy."

"But serenity is worth all these aggravations. It is the proper time. Let go of all your dislikes. Why are you like a donkey enduring the burden? Otherwise, you will always be slave to someone who can who can have you released or block your way. You will have to serve him as you would a devil."

There is only one way to be happy. Keep this thought ready for use morning, noon, and night. Give up the desire for things not under your control. Don't think of anything as your own. Hand over everything to fortune and the deity. Leave these things in the care of supervisors appointed by God. Meanwhile, you concern yourself with only one thing: what is your own and what is free from restrictions. When you read, read about this. Write about this. Listen about this.

Your judgement behind your action is what makes it good or bad

That's why I cannot call someone productive, if I hear he reads and writes all night long. I need to know why he is doing it. You wouldn't call a man productive if he loses sleep over a girl. Neither would I. If he loses sleep for fame, I would call him ambitious; if for money, greedy; but not productive. If he does it for the sake of his ruling faculty, to live well in accordance with nature, only then would I call him productive. You should never praise or blame a man for an action that may be good or bad, but for the reasons for his action – his judgement about it. Judgements are unique to each individual and they are what make one's action good or bad.

Be happy with the present

Knowing all this, be happy for what you have. Be satisfied with what each moment brings. If any of these things you studied and learned prove useful to you in your actions, be joyful. If you have got rid of or reduced your tendency to impulsiveness, indecent language, recklessness, laziness, and if you are not motivated by the same things that motivated you once, at least not to the same extent, then everyday becomes a festival: today because you acted well yesterday, tomorrow because you acted well today.

How much better reason is this for thanksgiving than a consulship or a governorship! These things come to you from your own self and from God. Remember who gave them, to whom, and why. If you are brought up to reason like this, how can you ever ask where you will be happy and where you will please God? No matter where they are, aren't people equally distant from God? And, no matter where they are, don't they all see the same thing?

Think about this

Don't be hard to please. Don't complain about trivial things. "The vinegar is bad, it's sharp; the honey is foul, it upsets my stomach; I don't like the vegetables. *Discourses IV.4.25. Epictetus*

CHAPTER 5

Freedom from Conflicts

Key ideas of this discourse

1. *A good person is not in conflict with anyone. If she can, she prevents others from getting into conflict.*
2. *When others make a mistake, remember things could be worse.*
3. *Different people judge things differently. This leads to conflict.*

A good person does not quarrel with anyone

A good and excellent person does not quarrel with anyone. To the extent he can prevent it, he does not allow others to quarrel, either. Socrates sets an example for this, as he did in many things. He not only did not quarrel with anyone, he also tried to prevent others from quarrelling. You can read about how many quarrels he ended in Xenephon's *Symposium*; how patient he was with [aggressive debaters such as] Thrasymchus, Polus and Callicles, and how he was habitually to his wife as well as his son when he tried to refute him. Why? Because Socrates knew very well that no one can control what was not his own and he desired only what was his own.

"And what's that?

"It is not trying to make the other person act according to their nature, because that's not within our power. While others act the way they think best, we continue to act according to our nature, minding only our own business in such a way that others may also may be in harmony with nature. This is what a good and excellent person should always try to."

"To hold high office?"

"No, but if it is offered to you, to preserve the right conduct of your ruling faculty."

"To marry?"

"No, but if it is offered to you, to keep yourself in accordance with nature."

Be glad that this is not the worst that could possibly happen

But if you wish that your son or wife never commit a mistake, you are wishing for things not your own. And getting an education means this: Learning what is your own and what is not your own. When you understand this, what's left to fight about? Then you will not be surprised by anything that comes about, will you? Will anything seem strange to you? Are you not prepared for worse and tougher things than what happens to you? Won't you count it as a blessing if things don't turn out as bad as they possibly could?

"So-and-so abused you."

"I'm grateful he didn't hit me."

"He hit you too."

"I'm grateful he didn't wound me."

"He wounded you too."

"I'm grateful he didn't kill me."

When, and in which school, did he ever learn that human beings are gentle, social animals and that injustice is harmful to the person who causes it? If he has not learned these things and is not convinced of them, why shouldn't he follow the course of action that seems to his advantage?

"My neighbour has thrown stones."

"Does that mean that *you* have done something wrong?"

"No, but things in my house have been broken."

Are you a piece of crockery then? No, but a person with a capacity to choose. So what resource do you have to counter this? If you think you are a wolf, then bite back and throw more stones. But if you ask me a question as a human being, examine the treasure you possess. Think what faculties you brought with you into this world. It is not the faculty of brutality, is it? It is not the faculty of bearing grudges, is it? When is a horse miserable? When he cannot do what he is born for: not when he cannot crow, but when he cannot run. A dog? Not when he cannot fly, but when he cannot hunt. Don't you think that the same principle applies to human beings too? Not when he cannot choke lions? Embrace statues (nature hasn't given anyone a special faculty for this)? No. Only when he has lost his kindness and trustworthiness.

This is the kind of person for whom all people should, "gather together to mourn because he has come into the world with so many evils." We don't mourn for the person who is born or for the person who dies but for a person who, while still alive, loses what is properly his own. We are not talking about his inheritance, his land, his house, or his staff and helpers. None of this is a man's own. They all belong to others, are slavish and controlled by others. The master [God] gives them now to one person, now to another. We mourn for the loss of his personal qualities as a human being, the imprints he brought with him when he entered the world. [The quotation in this paragraph is from a passage in Euripides' *Cresphontes,* as translated by Robin Hard.]

"Just as we accept the coin if it has the imprint of Trajan and reject it if it has the imprint of Nero, we look at the imprint of his judgements. What does it say?"

"He is gentle, generous, patient, and affectionate."

"Bring him to me. I will make him a fellow citizen and accept him as a neighbour and travelling companion. Just make sure that he doesn't have the imprint of Nero. Does he get angry quickly, is he malicious, and does look for faults in others?"

"If he feels like it, he punches the people he meets."

"Then why do you say he is a human being? You can't judge everything by outward appearance, can you? By outward criterion, you could call a ball of wax an apple.

No, the outward appearance alone won't do; for it to be an apple it should taste and smell like an apple. So also, neither are the eyes and the nose sufficient to prove that one is a human being. You must see if he also has proper judgements as a human being."

"Here is a person who doesn't listen to reason. He doesn't understand when he is proven wrong."

"He is an ass."

"Here's another who is completely shameless."

"He is worthless, a sheep. Anything but a human being."

"Here's a man looking for somebody to kick and bite."

"He's neither an ass nor a donkey, but some sort of wild beast."

"Then would you have others despise me too?"

"Despised by whom? By people of understanding? How can they despise someone who is gentle and modest?"

"By those who lack understanding, then?"

"What's that to you? Does a craftsman worry about people who don't understand his craft?"

"They would be even more ready to attack me."

"What do you mean by *me*? Can anyone hurt your choice? Can anyone stop you from interpreting impressions according to nature?"

"No."

Why are you, then, still bothered? Why do you want to show yourself to be timid? Why don't you come forward and say that you are at peace with all human beings, no matter what they do. And that you are amused at those who think they could harm you: "These slaves do not know who I am or where my good and evil lie. They can't touch what is truly my own." It is like the way citizens of a strong city laugh at those who surround the city to capture them. "Why do they bother? Our wall is secure, and we have provisions and other supplies for a long time." These are things that make a city strong and secure, just as human judgments make human souls secure.

What wall is so strong, what body is so steely, what property is safe against theft, and what reputation is so unassailable? All things everywhere are perishable and easily attacked and captured. Anyone who gets attached to any of them will necessarily be troubled, worry about the future, and be subjected to fear and sorrow. They are bound to become frustrated in their desires and fall into what they want to avoid. Given all this, aren't we willing to make secure the only way given to us that would lead us to safety? Aren't we willing to give up what is perishable and slavish and instead devote our efforts to what is imperishable and free by nature? And don't we remember that no one either harms or benefits another. Rather it is the judgement about these things that hurts and upsets a person.

Differences in judgement produce conflict

This is what gives rise to disagreements, inner conflict, and war. What made [*the famous enemy brothers*] Eteocles and Polynices enemies was nothing other than differences in judgments – about the throne and about the exile – namely, one was the greatest of all goods and the other, the greatest of all evils. This is the nature of every being: to pursue the good and avoid the bad. If someone makes us avoid the good and pursue the bad, then that person is an enemy and a traitor, even if he is a brother, a son, or a father, because nothing is more precious to us than the good.

If good and bad lie in externals, then there is no affection between father and son, brother and brother. All the world will be full of enemies, traitors, and informers. But if the right choice is the only good and the wrong choice is the only evil, where is any room for quarrels and defamations? About what? About the things that mean nothing to us? Against whom? Against the ignorant, the miserable and the most deceived about the most important things?

Socrates remembered all this when he lived in his house – putting up with an ill-tempered wife and an unkind son. How did she show her bad temper? By pouring on him as much water as she liked and by trampling his cake under her foot. And what is it to me, if I consider it nothing? But this choice of mine no one can hinder. No master, no tyrant. No single person or a crowd. In this, the stronger cannot stop the weaker, because it is a God-given right, free from restrictions.

Such judgments bring love to a household, harmony to a nation and peace among nations of the world. They make a person grateful to God and always confident, because what he is dealing with is not his own and, therefore, is of no value to him. We may be able write about these things and approve of them when we read about them, but we are not really convinced about them.

So, the proverb about the Spartans "Lions at home, but foxes at Ephesus," applies to us too. We are lions in the classroom but foxes outside. [The proverb refers to the fact that the Spartan military was successful in Greece but not Asia Minor where Ephesus is located.]

Think about this

A virtuous and good person neither quarrels with anyone, nor, as far he can, does he allow anyone else to quarrel. Don't be hard to please. Don't complain about trivial things. "The vinegar is bad, it's sharp; the honey is foul, it upsets my stomach; I don't like the vegetables. Discourses IV.5.1. Epictetus [RH]

CHAPTER 6

Freedom
from the Opinions of Others

Key ideas of this discourse

1. *There is no need to worry about what others say about you.*

2. *If others have things like money, office, and other things, it is because they worked for it.*

3. *When you work towards making better judgments, this is where you should look for an advantage over others. But you don't, because you don't fully believe that what you have is as valuable as what others have. Therefore, you're bothered by what others think of you.*

4. *Pay attention to what you truly care about. Then you won't be upset by what others think or say about you.*

There is no need to be upset if others pity you

[A student said to Epictetus]

"It annoys me when people pity me."

"Who's responsible for this? You or the people who pity you? Can you stop this from happening?"

"I can stop it, if I can show them that there is no reason for them to pity me."

"But is this something in your power – whether or not people pity you?"

"Yes, I think it is in my power. But people don't pity me for the right reasons, for my faults that deserve pity. Instead, they pity poverty, lack of office, illness or death, and other things like that."

"Then, are you ready to convince the world that none of these things are bad and that you can be happy even when you are poor, hold no office or honour? Or do you want show yourself off to them as a rich person and an official?"

If you choose the second option [of showing yourself off], then you are an egotist, a tasteless and worthless person. Think about what you must do to achieve this. You will have to borrow some workers, own silverware, and show them off in public often, each time making sure it looks different. You will need flashy clothes and all kinds of accessories. You should show yourself off as one who is honoured by distinguished people and try to dine with them or at least make others believe that you do. You need to treat your body such that it looks better looking and more distinguished than you really are. You need to follow all this if you want to follow the second option, so people don't pity you.

But the first option – convincing everyone what things are good and what things are bad – is both impractical and tedious. Even God himself couldn't do it. That power hasn't been given to you, has it? The only power given to you is to convince yourself and you are yet to do it. And you are trying to convince others?

You are not convinced yourself that what you have is good

Who has lived with you for as long as you have lived with yourself? Who could convince you as well as you could? Who is better disposed towards you and closer to you than you are to yourself? How is it then you have not convinced yourself of this? Isn't this upside down? Is this what you're concerned about? Is this what you're anxious about? And not about how to get rid of pain, chaos, and humiliation so you can be free? Haven't you heard that there is only one way to get there: to give up things that are outside your choice or control, to turn away from them and to admit that they are not your own?

"What kind of a thing is this then – someone else's opinion about you?"

"It is something outside my choice or control."

"Is it nothing to you, then?"

"Yes, it is nothing."

"If you are still stung and disturbed by the opinion of others, can you say you are fully convinced about what is good and bad? Why don't you let others alone, and become your own teacher and your own student? Let others think about whether it is in their interest to live according to nature, and live accordingly. But, as for you, no one is closer to you than yourself."

"I have heard philosophers say and agreed with them; yet I don't feel that my burden has lightened. What do you think it means?"

"Can it be that you are dull?"

"In other things I tried, I was not found to be dull. I learned to read and write quickly, learned wrestling and geometry, and learned how to analyse syllogisms."

"Can it be, then, that reason has failed to convince you?"

"But there is nothing that I approved more from the beginning, nothing that I preferred more; and now I spend my time reading, writing and, hearing about them. To this day, I have not found a stronger argument than this. What am I missing?"

"Can it be that you still have contradictory opinions? That you have not strengthened your convictions through exercises and have not yet got into the habit of testing your convictions with facts? Have you stored your convictions away like old, rusty pieces of armour that no longer fit you?"

"If I look at other things I have learned, such as wrestling, reading, and writing, I am not satisfied with just learning. I continue think about and analyse the arguments that are presented to me. And I construct new arguments, even equivocal arguments. But I don't exercise the necessary principles that will release me from fear, grief, passion, and hindrance and make me free; neither do I apply enough care to them. After all that, I am worried about what others will say of me. Will I appear important and happy in their eyes?"

"O miserable man, won't you see what you are saying about yourself? What kind of a person are you in your own eyes? What kind of a person are you in your thoughts, desires, and aversions? What kind of a person are you in your choices, preparations, and projects and all other human activities? Yet you are concerned with whether other people pity you?"

"Yes, because I don't deserve to be pitied."

"So, you are upset by that? If one is upset, then doesn't one deserve pity?"

"Yes."

"Then, how can you still say that you don't deserve pity? The way you feel about pity makes you worthy of pity."

Why should you care if what others say about you is not true?

Haven't you heard what [the philosopher] Antisthenes said: "It's a king's lot, Cyrus, to do well, and be spoken ill of."

My head is perfectly all right. What do I care if others think I have a headache? I have no fever, yet people sympathize with me as if I had one:

"Poor man, how long have you had this fever?"

So I put on a long face and say, "Yes, I have not been well for a long time."

"What will happen to you then?"

"Whatever God decides." At the same time, I'm secretly amused at those who pity me.

Why can't I do same thing when it comes to other things? I'm poor, but I have the right judgment on poverty. What is it to me if people pity me for my poverty? I don't hold office, while others do. But I have the right judgment about holding or not holding office. Let others pity me or look to their own, but I am not hungry, thirsty, or cold. Yet because they are hungry and thirsty, they think I am too. What should I do then? Go about announcing, "Don't be fooled, you people. It's all well with me. I pay no attention to poverty, lack of office, or anything else except for correct judgments, which I have without any restriction. I really don't think about other things." What nonsense is this? How can I have right judgment when I am not satisfied with who I am but feel upset about how I look to others?

If others have what you don't have, it's because they worked to get it

"But others will get more than I do, and be held in greater honour."

Isn't it reasonable that those who work towards an advantage should have it? They worked towards holding office, and you towards making correct judgments; they to wealth, you to judging your impressions the right way. What you should look at is whether they have an advantage over you on things you worked towards, but they didn't. Are their judgments in accordance with nature? Are they more successful in achieving their desires? Are they able to avoid what they don't want? Are they more certain of achieving their goals in their designs, purposes, and choices? Do they do what is fitting as human beings, as sons, as parents, and as designated in other relationships?

If they hold office and do everything to get it, and you don't hold office and don't do anything to get it, why don't you tell yourself the truth? Isn't it most unreasonable to expect a person who work towards something to be less successful than the one who doesn't?

"No, because I take trouble over right judgments, it is more reasonable for me to have the upper hand."

"Yes, in what you take trouble over – your judgements. But in those things that others have taken more trouble over than you, give way to them. Otherwise, it would be like expecting yourself to hit the target in archery, because you have correct judgments. Or expecting to surpass blacksmiths in their trade."

Pay attention to things you care about

So, stop taking your judgments so seriously. Pay attention to things that you care about. And then cry if you aren't successful in getting them, because then your crying is justified. But you say that you are busy with other things and are attending to those things. As people say, "One serious business has no partnership with another."

[This is a quote from Pythagoras' Golden Verses, as translated by William Oldfather.]

One person gets up at dawn and looks for someone who is close to a powerful person and salutes him; looks for someone with whom he can have a pleasant conversation or send a gift; thinks about ways to please a dancer; or how he may please someone by maligning someone else. Whenever he prays, he prays for things like these. Whenever he sacrifices, he sacrifices for things like these. He applies the saying, "Let not sleep descend on your weary eyes," by Pythagoras for these purposes. [Then he wonders] "Where did I go wrong in my flattery? What did I do? Could it be that I acted as a free and noble-minded person?" If he does find any such action he criticizes and accuses himself: "What did you do that for? Couldn't you have lied? Even philosophers say that nothing stops one from lying."

Ask yourself these questions

But if you have really paid attention to nothing else other than how to make right use of impressions, then, as soon as you get up in the morning, you should ask yourself:

- *What have I yet to do* to achieve freedom from passion? To achieve peace of mind?
- *What am I?* Am I just a worthless body? Am I property? Am I reputation? None of these.
- *What am I then?* I am a rational living being.
- *What then is expected of me?* Go over your actions in your mind.

- *Where have I gone wrong in achieving happiness?*
- *What did I do* that was unfriendly, unsociable, or inconsiderate?
- *What did I fail to do* that I ought to have done regarding these things?

Since people differ so greatly in their desires, actions and prayers, do you still expect to have equal share with them in those things to which they have devoted time, but you have not? Is it any surprise that they pity you and you are upset?

"But they are not worried if you pity them."

"Why not?"

"Because they are convinced that they are getting good things, but you are not so convinced. So, you are not happy with what you have and you want what they have. But, if you are truly convinced that what you have is good while they are mistaken, you would not care at all about what they say."

Think about this

If you were truly convinced that it is you who are in possession of what it good, and they are mistaken, you would not even have given a thought to what they say about you. Discourses IV.6.38 Epictetus [CG/RH]

CHAPTER 7

Freedom from Fear

Key ideas of this discourse

1. *You are afraid because you think you would lose things that you value – such as your body and your property.*
2. *If you stop caring about external things, no one can frighten you.*
3. *Align your desires with what actually happens in life.*
4. *External things are useless playthings. Turn your attention to useful things.*

Why you are afraid

"What makes a tyrant frightening?"

"His guards, his swords, his posse who shut the door on others."

"Well then, how is it a child is unafraid in his presence? Doesn't the child notice the guards? Suppose someone is fully aware of them and of their swords but has come precisely because he wants to die because of some misfortune. He is looking for an easy death at someone else's hands and he won't be frightened of the guards either, will he?"

"No, because he wants exactly what makes them frightening."

"Well then. If you don't particularly care whether you live or die, and are willing to accept whatever comes your way, what will stop you from facing a tyrant without fear?"

"Nothing."

"Suppose you felt the same way about your property, your wife, and your children – due to some madness or desperation – you would not value material things either. It would be like children playing with pieces of broken pottery, competing with other children in the game. What tyrant, what guards, what swords could still frighten you?"

If madness, or habit in the case of Galileans [Christians], can make people adopt such attitude toward these things, can't reason and demonstration teach people that God made everything in the universe? And that the universe is free from hindrance, self-sufficient, and every part of it serves the needs of the whole?

Align what you want with what happens

No other animal can understand nature's rule. But human beings are rational. They can think about these things and know that he is a part of them, the kind of part he is, and also to know it is all right for parts to work for the benefit of the whole. Human beings are noble by nature, high minded, and free rational animals. So, they notice that some things around them are free, unrestricted, and under their control, and others are not. What is within their control and choice is free and unrestricted. What is not within their choice and control is unfree and restricted.

Therefore, if you decide that your good and advantage lies only in things that are free and unrestricted and completely under your control, you will be free, peaceful, unharmed, high-minded, reverent, thankful to God for all things, never finding fault with anything or blaming anything.

On the other hand, if you decide that your good and advantage lie in external things that are outside you control, inevitably you will be hindered and restrained. You will be slavish to those who have control over the things that you so admire or fear. You will necessarily be disrespectful to God because you believe that He is harming you, unjust. You will be trying to claim more than your proper share and you are bound to become base and mean-spirited.

External things mean nothing

If you have understood these things, what is there to stop you from living light and living with ease, from gently awaiting anything that may happen, and being content with whatever might have happened?

Would you have me poor? Bring it on! Then you will see what poverty is when a good actor is playing the part.

Would you like have me hold office? Bring it on!

Would you like me *not* to hold office? Bring it on!

Would you like to me suffer hardships? Bring them on, too!

Would you like to banish me? Wherever I you ask me to go, I am well with it. Here, where I am now, is well with me, not because of location but because of my judgments. These judgements I will carry with me wherever I go. No one can take these away from me. Those are my only things, they cannot be taken away. I am content to have only those, wherever I am, whatever I do.

"But it is time for me to die."

What do you mean by "die" Don't talk about it as though it is a tragic thing, but the way it actually is: "It's time for the materials that you are made of to go back to where they came from." What is so terrible about that? Is the universe going to be any less because of that? Is anything new or unreasonable about to happen? Is this why you are afraid of bullies? Or of the weapons their bodyguards carry with them? Let others worry about those things. I have thought about them and no one is my master. God has set me free and I know his commands. No one can enslave me. I have the right liberator, and the right judges.

"Am I not the master of your body?"

"What's it to me then?"

"Am I not a master of your property?"

"What's it to me then?"

"Am I not the master of your exile and imprisonment?"

"I give you all these, and my body too, whenever you please. Test your power and see how far it goes. Who can I be afraid of now? The officials? What could they do, shut the door on me? Let them shut the door, if I want to enter it."

"Then why do you come to the door?"

"Because I think it is fitting for me to take part in the game as long as it lasts."

"Why aren't you shut out?"

"Because, if I am shut out, I have desire to go in. I always want what actually happens. God's judgement is better than my desires. I am his servant, his follower. His choice is my choice. His desire is my desire. His will is my will. No one can shut me out. Only a person who tries to force their way in can be shut out."

"Why don't you try to force your way in, then?"

"Because I know that nothing good is handed to those who force their way in."

No. When I hear that someone has been honoured by the head of the state, I ask, "What has he gained? Has he also gained the judgment needed to govern a province? Has he gained the capacity to carry out legal and administrative duties?" Why should I try to force my way in, then? Someone is scattering figs and nuts. The children scramble to pick them up and fight among themselves. But not grown-ups, because they think it is trivial. But if you scatter broken pieces of pottery, even children won't scramble to get them.

Externals are worthless

Governorships are available? Let children go after them.

Money? Let children go after it.

High offices? Let children fight and go after these, have doors shut on their face, let them take a beating, let them kiss the hand of the powerful and of their servants.

But, for me, they are just figs and nuts.

"What if, by chance, a fig lands on your lap?"

"I will pick it up and eat it. A fig has at least that much value. But no fig has that much value as to lowering yourself to get it, upsetting someone, being upset by someone, or flattering someone who can give it to me. The same is true of all those other things that are not any good and which philosophers have convinced me as being no good."

Show me the swords of the guards.

"See how big they are, and how sharp."

"What do they do, these big sharp swords?"

"They kill."

"And fever, what does it do?"

"The same thing."

"And a tile? What does it do?"

"The same thing."

"Would you then want me to be in awe of these things? Bow before them? Be a slave to them all?"

"Heaven forbid!"

Everything that's born must die, so the world may not stand still or may be blocked. Once I understood this, it made no difference to me whether I die by a fever, a tile, or a soldier. But, if I have to compare, I know that a soldier will bring it about relatively painlessly and quickly. Therefore, I know that I don't fear anything that a tyrant can inflict upon me. I also know that he doesn't have anything I want.

Then, why should I admire him? Why should I be in awe of him? Why should I be afraid of his guards? Why should I be happy if he speaks kindly to me and welcomes me? Why should I tell others about it? He's no Socrates, is he? He is no Diogenes either, is he? Then, is his praise any proof of what I am? I have not been eager to imitate his character, have I? No, but as a player in a game, I come to him and serve him, if he doesn't ask me to do something stupid or improper. But if he should say, "Go to Salamis and bring back Leo," I say, "Find someone else. I am not playing anymore." [For more on Leon and the Thirty Tyrants, see the first discourse in this book.] "Put him in jail," says the tyrant. I follow, it's all a game.

"But you'll lose your head."

"Is he going to keep his forever? Or, are you, who obey him?"

"You will be tossed out without a burial." [This is supposed to be an insult.]

"If I am the corpse, I will be thrown out. If I am not the corpse, speak more intelligently, in line with the facts and do not try to scare me."

Such things are frightening to children and fools. Once a person enters the school of a philosopher, and yet doesn't know himself, he deserves to be afraid. If he hasn't learned that he is not his flesh, bones, or sinews, but makes use of these, and governs and understands impressions, then he will flatter those he flattered before.

"But such arguments encourage people to despise the laws."

Yield to superior and stronger things

Quite the opposite. What arguments (other than these) would make people who follow them readier to obey laws? Law is not within the reach of any fool. And yet, see how these arguments lead us to behave the right way even towards these fools. They teach us not to claim anything in which they can surpass us. They teach us to give way when it comes to our poor body, our property, our children, our parents and our brothers; to give up everything and let everything go. There is only one exception to this: our judgments. They are accordance with nature and it is each person's special property. What is unreasonable about this? What law did I break? Where you are stronger and superior, I give way to you. So also, where I am superior, you give way to me.

You excel in what you care about

I care about these things, but you don't. What you care about is how to live in marble halls, how to be served by your staff and servants, how to wear fine clothes, how to have a variety of hunting dogs, musicians, and entertainers at your beck and call. Do I ever care about any of these things? Have you ever, on the other hand, cared about judgments? Or about reason? You don't know, do you, about its different parts, how they are related to one another, how they are ordered, what it is capable of and what its nature is? Then why are you disturbed if someone else who has studied these things has the advantage over you in these matters?

"But these *are* the most important things."

What stops you, then, from turning your attention to them? And who has better resources – books, time and people to help – than you? You only need to pay attention to these matters some day and spend a little time understanding your ruling faculty. Think about what is this faculty that you have, where it came from, how it puts everything to the test and then accepts or rejects.

But so long as you concern yourself with externals, you will have those, in ways that no one else can match. And you will have this ruling faculty the way you want it – dirty and neglected.

Think about this

Once I come to learn that all that comes into being must also perish so the universe may not come to a standstill or be impeded, it no longer matters to me whether a fever brings that about, or a roof tile, or an armed guard. Discourses III.7.27. Epictetus [RH]

CHAPTER 8

Freedom from Hasty Judgments

Key ideas of this discourse

1. *Actions are neutral. What makes them good or bad is the judgment on which they were based.*
2. *Don't be carried away be external appearances and make hasty judgments.*
3. *What a person does is more important than what he claims he is.*
4. *If you want to make progress, train yourself and be patient. Don't try to show off before you are ready.*

What makes an action good or bad is the judgment behind it

Never praise or blame a person for things that may be either good or bad; don't think of it as evidence of that person's skill or lack of it. This way, you will escape hasty judgment and malice.

"He washes quickly."

"Is this, therefore acting badly?"

"No, not at all."

"What's he doing then?"

"He washes quickly."

"So, it is all right then?"

"No, that doesn't follow. [*No conclusion about right and wrong can be drawn by his act. His actions themselves are indifferent, and we do not know the reason behind his actions to make a judgement.*] If his action is the result of correct judgment, then it is good. If it is the result of bad judgment, it is bad. So, until you know a person's judgement behind their actions, you should neither praise nor criticize their actions."

Now, you cannot decide easily the nature of judgment behind an action by outward appearances.

"He is a carpenter."

"Why?"

"He's using a carpenter's tool."

"What does that prove?"

"She is a musician because she's singing."

"What does that prove?"

"He is a philosopher."

"Why?"

"Because he is wears rough clothes and has long hair."

So too do tramps. For that reason, if you find someone with that clothing and hair misbehaving, you should not immediately say, 'Look at that philosopher misbehaving!'. You should rather say, based on the person's misbehaviour, 'Look at that person. He is no philosopher at all.' If you think all that defines a philosopher is wearing rough clothes and sporting long hair, then you'd be right. But if you think of a philosopher as someone who is free from error, why do they not take away his designation as a philosopher when he doesn't behave like one?

Don't blame the profession because of a bad professional

This is not how you judge other professions. If you find someone shaping wood clumsily with an axe, you don't say, "What's the use of carpentry? See how bad a carpenter is." Instead you say, "He is no carpenter. He is bad handling an axe." Similarly, if you hear someone singing badly, you don't say, "Look, how musicians sing," but rather, "She's no musician." It is only regarding philosophy that people have this attitude. If someone behaves in a way that conflicts with the requirements of their profession, they don't refuse him the title of philosopher. Instead, they take him to be one and his misbehaviour as evidence of philosophy serving no useful purpose.

"Why?"

"Because we pay some attention to our conception of a carpenter or musician, but not to that of philosopher. Because our conception is confused and vague, we judge a philosopher by external appearances alone."

What other art requires one to adopt just costume and hairstyle but has no principles, subject matter, and aim?

"So, what is the subject matter of a philosopher? Is it rough clothes?"

"No, it is reason."

"What's his aim? To wear rough clothes?"

"No, but to reason correctly."

"What are his principles? To grow a long beard and thick hair?"

"No. Rather, as Zeno says, to understand the elements of reason and their nature, how they fit with one another and what comes out of all these facts."

Then, why don't you first examine whether a philosopher is true to his profession by misbehaving before accusing the profession itself? As it stands, because he seems to you to be acting badly while you are acting decently, you say, "Look at that philosopher!" as though it is proper to call a person behaving that way a philosopher. And then you say, "Is that what being a philosopher means?" But you don't say "Look at that carpenter!" or "Look at that musician!" when you know one of them is an adulterer and you see them eat like a glutton.

So, to a certain degree, you do see what a philosopher's profession is, but you slip up and get confused by your own carelessness.

Don't get carried away
by external appearances

But even those we call philosophers pursue their profession by means that may be sometimes good and sometimes bad. The moment they put on a philosopher's cloak and grow a beard they declare, "I'm a philosopher!" Yet no one says that she's a musician the moment she buys a musical instrument. No one says that he is a blacksmith because he has put on a felt cap and apron. No, they get their titles from their art, not from their clothes.

It is for this reason that [philosopher who dressed conventionally] Euphrates said,

"For a long time, I tried to hide the fact that I was a philosopher, and this worked for me. First, whatever I did, I did for my own sake and not for the sake of those watching me. It was for me that I ate properly, looked calm in the way I looked and moved. All this was for me and my God. Also, the contest was mine alone and so were the risks. If I did anything shameful or improper, it did not affect the cause of philosophy; I didn't commit faults as a philosopher. So those who did not know my intention used to wonder why I never became a philosopher, even though I knew all philosophers and lived with them. And where is the harm when people discover me as a philosopher because of what I do rather than by the way I dress?"

So, if you know how, judge me by all this: How I eat, how I sleep, how I endure, how I refrain, how I help, how I deal with my desires and aversions, how I preserve my relationships – natural or acquired, without confusion and without obstruction. But if you are so deaf and blind that you cannot even recognize [the divine patron of blacksmiths] Hephaestus as a good blacksmith without a felt cap on his head, where is the harm in not being recognized by so foolish a judge?

This is how most people failed to recognize Socrates for what he was. They would come and ask him to introduce them to philosophers. Was he irritated by them, as we should be, and say, "What! Don't *I* look like a philosopher to you?" No, he would take them to other philosophers and introduce them. He was satisfied with just being a philosopher and was happy that he wasn't annoyed by people not recognizing him as one. He always kept in mind his true business. What is the function of a good and excellent person? To have many pupils? Not at all. Let those who have made it their aim look to that. Is it to explain difficult theories precisely? Let others look to it too.

In what area, then, was he someone of note and wanted to be so? In an area where there was hurt and help. He said, "If someone can hurt me, then I am achieving nothing. If I wait for somebody to help me, I amount to nothing. If I want something and it doesn't happen, then I am miserable." It is in this great arena that he challenged others to engage with him and, in my opinion, did not give in to anyone. In what way, do you think? Was it by proclaiming and saying, "I am such and such a man."? Far from it. It was *being* such and such a man.

Judge people by their actions, not by what they say they are

It is the part of a fool and show-off to say, "I am tranquil and serene. Don't be ignorant, you people, while you are agitated and confused over things of no value, I alone am free from all disturbance." So, it is not enough for you to be pain free without also declaring "Come here, all of you who suffer from gout, or headache, or fever, or are lame, or blind and see how free I am from every disorder!" This is boastful and vulgar, unless you could show, like Asclepius [the son of Apollo], how they could treat all their ills and you are showing off your health as a proof of it.

Such is the course followed by the Cynic deemed worthy of receiving the sceptre and crown of Zeus and says,

"So, you may see, all mankind, you are seeking happiness and peace of mind not where it is, but where it is not. Behold, God has sent me to you as an example. I have no property, no house, no wife, no children, not even a bed, tunic, or furniture. See how healthy I am. Test me. If you see I am free from turmoil, hear my remedies and the treatment that cured me."

Now that is humane and noble. But see whose work it is. It is the work of God, or the work of someone deemed worthy by God, such that he may never lay bare anything before people that would undermine him as the witness for virtue and against external things.

His fair features never paled, nor from his cheeks Ever wiped he a tear. [*Homer,* Odyssey, *11.529-1, CG/RH*]

And not only this, he must neither yearn for something, nor seek after it – be it a person, place or a lifestyle – like children seeking after the vintage season or holidays. He must surround and adorn himself on every side with self-respect, as others do with walls, doors, and door-keepers.

But, as it stands, people are drawn towards philosophy like people with acid indigestion are drawn towards foods that they soon cannot stand. Then they set off after the sceptre, the kingdom. They let their hair grow long, put on rough clothes, bare their shoulder, and argue with everyone they meet. If they find someone with an overcoat, they quarrel with that person.

Train hard before you can blossom

Man, take a hard winter training first. Look at your own choices to see if they aren't those of a person with indigestion, or of a woman with the cravings of pregnancy. Practice so you don't let people know who you are at first. Keep your philosophy to yourself for a while. This is how fruit is produced: the seed must be buried and hidden for a season; it must then grow slowly to perfection.

But if it heads out before the stalk is properly jointed, it never matures, as with the plants in a garden of Adonis. ["Plants in a garden of Adonis" is proverbial saying for incompleteness and early fading.] Now you are like this plant. You have bloomed before your time and will wither in winter. See what farmers say about seeds when the hot weather comes early. They are worried that the seeds will grow lush, only to be destroyed in a single frost, exposing their weakness.

You should be careful, man. You have grown lush. You have leaped forward and gained some reputation before its due time. As a fool among fools, you think that you are somebody. You will be bitten by the frost; rather you have already been bitten by the frost down at the root. [A preposterous metaphor according to W.A. Oldfather since protected roots are not frostbitten ahead of the exposed parts of the plant.] You will still blossom a little at the top and think that you are still alive and flourishing.

Allow *us* at least to ripen as nature wishes. Why do you expose us to elements, why force us? We are not yet ready to face open air. Let the root grow, let it acquire the first joint, then the second, and then the third. Then, finally, the fruit will force its way out, even if I don't want it to. Who that has conceived and is full of such great judgments can be unaware of his own nature and resources? Will he not be in a hurry to act according to them? Why, a bull is not unaware of its nature and resources when some wild beast comes along and does not wait for somebody to encourage him. Not does a dog, when he sees some wild animal.

If I possess the resources of a good person, shall I wait for you to come up and equip me for my proper work? But, believe me, I don't have them yet. Why then would you have me wither away before my time, just as you have done?

Think about this

Until you learn the judgment from which a man performs each separate act, neither praise his action nor blame it.
Discourses IV.8.3. Epictetus [WO]

CHAPTER 9

Freedom from Following the Wrong Course

Key ideas of this discourse

1. *When you see someone with things you don't have don't envy. Think of what you have in their place.*
2. *By craving things that are of no value, you lose things that are of value.*
3. *It is easy to reverse the wrong course of action, once you see the value in doing so.*
4. *If you don't see any value in reversing the wrong course, not even God can help you.*

Do not envy what others have; you have something else

When you see someone in power, compare it to the benefit you have by not wanting it. When you see someone rich, see what you have instead of riches. If you don't

97

have anything in their place, you would be miserable. But if you have the advantage of not needing riches, know that you have something more than what the other person has, and of far greater value. Someone has an attractive spouse; you, the happiness of not desiring one.

Do you think these are trivial things? And what would these same people – the rich and powerful with attractive spouses – give to be able to look down upon riches and power, and those attractive spouses whom they love and win? Don't you know how thirsty someone gets who is feverish? It has no resemblance to that of a healthy person. A healthy person drinks and her thirst is gone. But a sick person feels all right for a while, feels nauseous, turns water into bile, vomits, bellyaches, and is even thirstier than before.

By craving things, you lose the valuable things you have

It is much the same to have money and yet crave it, have power and yet crave it, sleep with an attractive person and yet crave her – there will be jealousy, fear of loss, shameful words, thoughts, and deeds.

"And what do I lose?"

You were modest before. Now you are not. Have you lost nothing? Instead of Chrysippus and Zeno, you now read [the erotic writers] Aristides and Euneus. Have you lost nothing then? Instead of Socrates and Diogenes, you have come to admire a man who can seduce and corrupt the largest number of women. You want to be handsome (although you are not) and make yourself up and want show off your bright clothes to attractive women. You consider yourself lucky if you come across a good perfume anywhere.

But formerly you did not think of these things but only where you might find a decent discourse, a worthy person, and a noble thought. For this reason, you used to sleep like a man, appear in public as a man, wear men's clothes, and hold discourses worthy of a man. After all this do you still say that you have lost nothing? Is it just small change to lose self-respect and decency? Or do you think these things count for nothing? Perhaps, to you, these things no longer look serious. But there was a time when you thought it the only serious loss and harm and you were most anxious that nobody should drive you away from such thoughts and actions. Now you have been driven from such thoughts, not by others, but by yourself.

It is easy to correct yourself

Fight against yourself and regain your decency, self-respect, and freedom. If anyone ever told you about me that someone was forcing me to commit adultery, to wear clothes like yours, to wear perfume, would you not have gone and murdered the man who was mistreating me this way? Now, aren't you willing to come to your own rescue? And how much easier it is to rescue yourself! You don't have to kill, put in jail, or attack anyone. You don't have to come into the open, but only talk to yourself, someone who will be readily persuaded and to whom no one can be more persuasive than yourself.

So, first judge your actions. When you have condemned them, do not give up on yourself. Don't act like spiritless people who, once they give in, abandon themselves completely and are swept off by the current. Instead, learn from gymnastic trainers: Has the boy fallen down? "Get up and wrestle again until you get strong." You should also react in some similar way. You should know there is nothing more flexible than the human mind. You only to have to will a thing; it happens and it is set right. On the other hand, you only have to doze off and all is lost. Both destruction and deliverance come from within.

If you don't see the value of this, no one can save you

"What good do I get after all that?"

What greater good than this are you looking for? Instead of shameless, you will become self-respecting. Instead of faithless, you will be trustworthy; instead of self-indulgent, self-controlled. If you are looking for anything greater than these things, go on acting as you do now. Even God can no longer save you.

Think about this

Fight against yourself, vindicate yourself for decency, for respect, for freedom. Discourses. IV.9.11. Epictetus [WO]

CHAPTER 10

Freedom from Anxieties

Key ideas of this discourse

1. *When you are anxious about the future, you are mostly concerned with what is not under your control.*
2. *By thinking about what is not under your control, you let go of things that are under your control.*
3. *You don't have to be anxious. Either you'll adjust to the new reality, or find ways of coping with it using what is under your control. If all else fails, you can exit this world.*
4. *You can get rid of your anxieties by paying attention to what is under your control.*

Don't be anxious about the future

People find our difficulties and perplexities in external things.

"What shall I do?"

"How will it happen?"

"What will happen?"

"I am worried this will happen. Or, that will happen."

All these are said by people who are concerned about what is outside their control or choice. After all, who says, "How I am to make sure that I don't agree with something that's not true?"

If someone is so naturally gifted as to worry about things like these, I will remind her:

"Why are you anxious? It's in your own power. Be secure. Don't rush to agree with something you have not put to the test using the rule of nature."

Again, if you are anxious about your desire for fear that it would be incomplete or miss its mark; or about your aversion, for fear that you would fall into it, I would first give you a kiss of congratulation, because you've put aside things that excite others and their fears. You have turned your serious thoughts to your own true business, where your true self lies. After that, I will say to you, "If you always want to fulfil your desire, and always avoid what you do not want, do not desire anything that is not your own and do not be put off by anything that is not under your control. Otherwise, you must necessarily be bound to fail in achieving your desires and fall into what you want to avoid. Where is the difficulty here? Where is the room for, 'How it will it turn out'? Or for, 'Will this happen to me or that?'"

If it is outside your area of choice, it is nothing to you

"Is what happens in the future outside the area of your choice?"

"Yes."

"Does the essence of good and evil lie within your area of choice?"

"Yes."

"Is it in your power, then, to use whatever turns out according to nature?"

"Yes."

"Can anyone stop you?"

"No, no one."

"Then don't ask me anymore 'How will it turn out?' However it turns out, you will make good use of it and the outcome will be a blessing for you."

Tell me, what would Heracles have been if he had said, "What I can I do to stop a huge lion or a huge boar or savages from coming my way?" And why do you care? If a huge boar comes your way, you'll struggle more; if evil people, you'll rid of the world of evil people.

If it becomes unbearable, there's always a way out

"Perhaps. But what if I die doing so?"

"You will die a good person, performing a noble action. You must die anyway doing something or the other

– farming, digging, trading, holding a high office, suffering from indigestion or dysentery."

What would you want to be doing when death finds you? As far as I am concerned, I would wish it to be something suitable for a human being, some charitable, public spirited, or noble action. But if I cannot be caught doing anything as great as that, then I should like at least to be doing something that cannot be obstructed and which is proper for me to do: correcting myself, perfecting the faculty that corrects false impressions, and working to achieve calm while fulfilling my social duties. If I am so lucky, advancing to the third division of philosophy dealing with making judgments with confidence.

If death finds me occupied with these things, it is enough for me if I can lift up my hands to God and say,

"I have not neglected the faculties I received from you to understand and follow your rule. I have not dishonoured you, as far as it was in my power. See how I have used my senses and my preconceptions. Have I ever blamed you? Have I ever been dissatisfied with anything that came about, and wished it otherwise? Have I ever violated my social relationships? I am thankful to you for bringing me into this world. I am grateful for the things you have given me. I am content with the length of time I have enjoyed their use. Take them back again and assign them whatever place you wish. They are all yours and you gave them to me."

[*These imaginary last words of Epictetus were criticized by Elizabeth Carter, the first English translator of Epictetus' works, for being too immodest and lacking in humility.*

However, William Oldfather, an authoritative translator, believes otherwise. He points out that Epictetus did not say, "because I can lift up my hands to God and say...", but, "if I can lift up my hands to god and say...," which has a very different meaning.]

Isn't it enough to make one's exit in such a state of mind? And what life could be better than this, more fitting than of someone who thinks this way, and what end could be happier?

But for this to happen, you must accept no small troubles and make so small sacrifices. You cannot wish for a high office and this at the same time. You cannot be eager to own land and this as well; or worry about you or those who work for you. No. If you wish for anything that is not your own, you'll lose what is your own.

Nothing can be had without paying the price

This is the nature of things: Nothing can be had without paying the price. Why are you surprised? If you want influential office, you must stay up late, run back and forth, kiss hands, pine away at people's doors, say and do many things unsuited for a free person, send gifts to many people and daily presents to some. And what do you get for all this? Twelve bundles of rods, to sit three or four times on the tribunal, to give games in the Circus, and distribute lunches in little baskets. [*These are marks of a Roman consul.*] Show me if there is more to office than this.

For calm, for peace of mind, for sleeping when you are asleep, for being awake when you are awake, to be afraid of nothing, and to be anxious about nothing, are you unwilling to make any sacrifice or any effort? But, while you are engaged in all this, if you lose something that belongs to you, or spend to no purpose, or if someone got what you should have got, are you going to get upset immediately? Won't you balance what you are getting in return for what, how much in return for how much? Do you honestly expect to get things of such value for nothing? And how can you? One business has nothing to do with another.

You cannot devote your efforts both to getting external things and, at the same time, to your own ruling faculty. If you want the former, let the latter go. Otherwise, you will have neither the former nor the latter because you will be pulled in two different directions.

If you want the latter, let the former go. You'll spill oil, you'll lose your furniture, and you'll be calm. Fire will break out while you are away, your books will be destroyed but you'll deal with impressions according to nature.

You will always have options in the future

"But, I'll have nothing to eat."

"If you are in such a bad spot, dying is an option. This is the harbour where everyone ends up and this is our refuge. As a result, nothing that happens to us in life is difficult. You can leave the house whenever you want and no longer be bothered by the smoke."

Why are you anxious, then? Why do you stay awake at night? Why don't you calculate where your good and evil lie and say, "Both are under my control. Nobody can take one away from me and force me into the other." Why don't you then go to sleep and snore? All that's your own is safe. As for what is not your own, it will be the concern of those who get it, given to them by He who has the authority to give it. Who are you to wish that it should be this way or that? You have not been given that choice, have you?

Be satisfied with those things that are under your control. Make the best you can of them. As for the rest, let them be as their master pleases.

If you have these principles before your eyes, will you lie awake at night and toss from side to side? What do you wish for? What do you long for? For Patroclus, or Antilochus, or Potesilaus? [These are close friends of Herecules, who had died.] For when did [Hercules] imagine that his friends were immortal? When did he not have before his eyes that he or his friends must die, either the following day or the day after?

"Yes, but I thought he'd survive me and bring up my son."

"Because you're a fool. You are counting on things that are uncertain. Why don't you then blame yourself, instead of sitting here, crying like a baby."

"Yes, but he used to put out food for me."

"Because he was alive then, you idiot. Now he is dead. But Antomedon [charioteer for Achilles and Patroclus] will see to your needs. If he also should die, you'll find someone else."

If your cooking pot should break, would you die of hunger? Wouldn't you send out for a new pot?

"No, because no greater evil could ever afflict me." [Homer]

"Is this what you call evil, then? And, instead of getting rid of it, are you blaming your master for not warning you about it so you could go on spending all your time grieving?"

What do you think? Didn't Homer write these lines for us to see that there is nothing to prevent even those of the highest birth, the strongest, the wealthiest, and the most handsome from becoming miserable and utterly unhappy, if they hold incorrect judgements?

Think about this

If you wish for anything that is not your own, what is really your own will be lost. Discourses IV.10.19. Epictetus [RH]

CHAPTER 11

Freedom from Impurities

Key ideas of this discourse

1. *Cleanliness is a human trait.*
2. *The first purity is the purity of the mind.*
3. *But we should keep our bodies clean as well.*
4. *You will be credible when your physical appearance supports you.*
5. *Beautify your inner qualities, but don't neglect your outer appearance*

Cleanliness is a human trait

Some people question whether the social instinct is a necessary element of human nature. Even these people, it seems to me, would not question that the instinct of cleanliness is distinctly human and humans are distinguished from animals in this quality as much as by anything. [*William Oldfather comments that Epictetus is not correct in saying this since animals such as cats, moles, and snakes keep themselves as clean as any human being. Some animals are, in fact, as clean or cleaner than human beings.*] So, when we see some animal cleaning itself we are surprised and say that the animal is acting "like a human being." If we find some animal being dirty, we immediately say, "Well, of course it isn't a human being."

Thus, we think of cleanliness as a distinctly human quality, which we first received from the gods. Since gods are by nature pure and unsoiled, to the extent humans are close to the gods by way of reason, to that extent humans are pure and clean. But human beings, by nature, cannot be very pure because of the material they are made of. Their rationality given to them by the gods tries to keep it as clean as possible.

The first purity is the purity of the mind

The first and the highest purity is what develops in the mind. The same is true of bodily impurity. But you would not find the impurity of the body to be the same as that of the mind. What could make the mind more impure than what soils it regarding carrying out its own actions? Now the actions the mind is to exercise are

- choice and refusal;
- desires and aversions; and
- preparations, intentions, and assents.

What is it, then, that makes the mind dirty and impure in these actions? Nothing other than its bad judgments. So, the impurity of the mind consists of its bad judgments, and the purity of mind consists of creating within it the right judgments. A pure mind is, therefore, one that makes right judgments. That kind of mind alone can escape confusion and pollution of its own actions.

We should keep our bodies clean as well

We should try, as far as possible, to achieve something like this for our body too. It is impossible not to have some flow of mucus, because we are made that way. For that reason, nature has created hands and has made our nostrils like tubes to carry away the fluids. So, if anyone sniffs them up again, I say he isn't acting as a human being should.

"It's impossible for the feet not to get muddy and dirty when we pass through things of that kind."

"So, nature has provided us with water and with hands."

"It's impossible that some impurity from eating should not remain on the teeth."

"Nature says 'wash your teeth.'"

"Why?"

"So that you may be a human being and not a wild beast or a pig."

"It's impossible that through our sweat and the pressure of our clothes, some uncleanliness should not be left behind on our body that needs to be cleaned."

"For this reason we have water, oil, hands, a towel, a scraper, and everything else that is used for cleaning the body. Not in your case? But a smith will remove the rust from his iron, and has tools made for that purpose. You yourself wash your plate before you eat, unless you are hopelessly dirty and unclean. But will you not wash your body and keep it clean?"

"Why should I?"

"Let me say it again. First, to act like a human being and second, not to offend those whom you meet. You are doing something like this here, without realizing it. You think it is all right to smell bad. But do you think it is also all right for those who sit with you, those who recline by you at table, and those who kiss you?"

Oh, go off to into some backwoods, that's what you deserve. Spend your life there alone, smelling yourself. It is only right that you enjoy your uncleanliness all by yourself. But you are living in a city. What kind of character are you exhibiting when you behave without thought or consideration?

If nature has given you a horse under your care, would you have totally ignored it? Well then, think of your body as a horse that's entrusted to you. Wash it, rub it down, make it such that no one will turn their back on you or try to avoid you. But who doesn't want to avoid someone who is dirty and smelly, whose skin looks even worse than someone who is smeared with dung? In the latter case, the stench is external and accidental, but in your case, it is because of your neglect and, therefore, comes from within, as though you have grown completely rotten.

"But Socrates rarely bathed."

"And yet his body looked radiant. He was so agreeable and pleasing that the most handsome and noble were taken with him. They wanted to sit with him rather than with those with the finest features. He might have never bathed or washed, if he so pleased. Yet even his rare baths were effective."

"But Aristophanes says, 'I speak of pallid men who go barefoot.'"

"Yes, but he also says that Socrates 'walked on air' and stole people's clothes at the wrestling school. [*That is to say that Aristophanes' evidence is of no value.*] Yet all those who have written about Socrates say exactly the opposite: He was not just pleasant to listen to, but pleasant to look at. They have written the same about Diogenes, too."

You will be credible when your physical appearance supports you

Even by the way we look, we shouldn't do anything to scare people away from philosophy. In our body, as in everything else, we should show ourselves to be appealing and untroubled. "Look, people. I have nothing, and I need nothing. I have no house and no city and am a refugee, if it so happens, and have no hearth. Yet, see how I live a happier and a more untroubled life than all the noble and the rich. Yes, and you can see how even my poor body is not injured by my plain living."

But if someone with the appearance and expression of a condemned person tells me this, what god will persuade me to come near philosophy, if those are the sorts of people philosophy produces? It is not for me. I would not do it. Not even if it would make me a wise person.

I'd rather have young people who are just beginning to feel drawn towards philosophy come to me with hair well-dressed rather than dishevelled and dirty. For it shows that here is a young person with a certain sense of beauty and a desire for elegance, and where he sees it, he cultivates it. And all I have to do is to show him the way, and say, "Young man, you're seeking the beautiful, and you'll do well. Know then, it comes from your reasoning faculty. Look for it there where you have your impulses to act or not to act, where you have desires and aversions. This part is something special you have within you, but your body is nothing but clay. Why trouble yourself about it for no purpose? If you learn nothing else, time will at least teach you that it is nothing."

But if he comes to me soiled and dirty, with moustaches down to his knees, what can I say to him? What sort of comparison can I give to convince him? What has he ever concerned himself with that is beautiful, so I can redirect his attention and say, "Beauty not there, but here."? Do you want me to tell him, "Beauty does not lie in being soiled and dirty, but in reason."? Does he care for beauty? Does he show any sign of it? Go and argue with a pig that it should not wallow in mud! It was for this reason that the discourses of Xenocrates appealed even to Polemo, a young man who loved beauty. He had come to Xenocrates with the first glimmers of enthusiasm for the beautiful, though he was looking for it in the wrong place. [*Polemo, the head of the Platonic Academy and the teacher of Zeno was converted to philosophy by Xe-nocrates, the previous head of the Academy. See Discourses 3.11]*

As a matter of fact, nature has not made dirty even the animals which associate with humans. Does a horse wallow in mud? Or a well-bred dog? But the pig, filthy geese, worms, and spiders – the creatures farthest removed from humans – do. Do you not then, a human being, want to be even among the animals that associate with humans, but rather be a worm or a spider? Will you not take a bath somewhere, sometime in any way you like? Will you not wash yourself? If you don't like hot water, then use cold. Will you not come to us clean, that your companions may be happy. What, do you even enter our temples that way, where it is forbidden by custom to spit or blow one's nose, when you yourself are nothing more than spit and drivel?

Beautify your inner qualities, but don't neglect your outer appearance

Well, what then? Is anyone demanding that you make yourself beautiful? By no means, except in those things that nature requires: the reason, its judgments, and its activities. But with regards to your body, only so far as cleanliness demands, to avoid offending others. If you hear that one shouldn't wear purple, go off, smear your cloak with dung or tear it to pieces.

"Where can I find rough clothes that look good?"

"Man, you have water, wash it. Look, here's a lovable young man, here is an old man worthy of love and to be loved in return. Here is someone to whom one can entrust the education of one's son; to whom perhaps daughters and young men will come – all to having him deliver his lectures from dung-hill! Heavens, no!"

Every eccentricity is the result of some human trait. But this comes close to not being human at all.

Think about this

Is anyone demanding that you beautify yourself? Heaven forbid! except that you beautify that which is our true nature – the reason, its judgments, and its activities; but your body, only so far as cleanliness only so far as to keep it cleanly; only so far as to avoid giving offence. Discourses IV.11.33. Epictetus [WO]

CHAPTER 12

Freedom
from Mind Wandering

Key ideas of this discourse

1. *When you let your mind wander, you can't bring it back whenever you like*
2. *You should constantly keep the basic principles at hand.*
3. *Practice the basic principles. Don't worry about pleasing others.*
4. *You don't need to be perfect. But don't procrastinate. Procrastination can only lead to more procrastination.*

When you let your mind wander,
you can't bring it back whenever you like

When you relax your attention for a short while, don't imagine that you can get it back whenever you like. Remember, because of your mistake today, your future conditions will necessarily be worse. The primary and the

most important thing is this: First you develop the habit
of not paying attention. Next you develop the habit of
deferring attention. Then you get into the habit of putting off time after time the happy and appropriate way of
life that is, and will be, in accordance with nature. If putting it off is advantageous, giving it up completely should
be even better. But if it is not, why don't you maintain
your attention continuously?

"I want to play today."

"What's there to stop you from playing with attention?"

"I want to sing."

"What's there to stop you from singing with attention?"

Surely, there's no area of life that's not covered by attention. Is there anything that you will do better by not
attending than by attending? Is there anything at all in
life that's not done better by those who pay attention
than by those who don't? Does an inattentive carpenter
do a more accurate job? Does an inattentive helmsman
steer more safely? is there any less important function
that can be done better by not paying attention?

Don't you see that when your let your mind wander,
it is no longer within your power to bring it back, either
to dignity, or to self-respect, or to good order? But you
do everything that comes into your head and you follow
your impulses.

What you should constantly attend to

"What should I attend to, then?"

"First, the general principles. You should have them at your command, and should not go to sleep, or get up, or drink, or eat, or mingle without these principles:

No one is a master of another's choice.

In choice alone our good and evil lie.

No one has the power to secure you in any good or involve you in any evil.

You alone have the authority over yourself in these matters.

Since these things are secure for you, why do you have to trouble yourself with externals? What bully can intimidate you? What disease? What poverty? What obstacle?

"But I haven't pleased so-and-so."

"Is he an action of yours, then?"

"No."

"Is he your judgement?"

"No."

"Why do you bother about him any further, then?"

"But he is highly thought of."

"Let him and those who think highly of him see to that. But you have one whom you must please, whom you must submit to, whom you must obey – that is God and, after that, yourself. He has entrusted you to yourself and made your choice subject to yourself alone, and gave you rules for the right use of it. When you follow these rules, don't pay attention to anyone who argues from equivocal premises."

Why then do you get you annoyed with those who are critical of you in these most important matters? Why should you be troubled in that way? For no other reason except that you lack training in this area. Every science has a right to despise ignorance and ignorant people. Not only the sciences, but arts and crafts as well. Take any shoemaker, take any smith you like, and he laughs at the rest of the world with regard to his own business. This is true of carpenters as well.

Practice these principles

Therefore,

- First of all, we keep these principles at hand and do nothing without them; keep our mind directed to this purpose; go after nothing external, nothing not our own; rather – as the one with authority has ordained – pursue without reservation things that are within the area of our choice, and other things only as far as they are given to us.

- Next, we must remember who we are, what our role is, and try to act appropriately as our social relationships require.

- We must remember what is the proper time to sing, the proper time to play, and in front of whom; what will be out of place, so our companions won't look down upon us, and we don't look down upon ourselves. When we joke, whom we laugh at; to what purpose to engage in social relations and with whom; and, finally, how to preserve our own character.

Whenever you deviate from any of these rules, you immediately suffer loss. It is not from anything external, but from your own action.

You can't be perfect, but no need to procrastinate

So, is it possible to be altogether faultless? No, that is unrealistic. But it *is* possible to strive continuously to avoid faults. We must be content, by never relaxing our attention, if we manage to escape at least a small number of faults. But now, when you say, "I will begin to pay attention tomorrow," let me tell you what you mean: "Today, I will be shameless, tactless, and mean-spirited. Other people can cause me distress. I will get angry and I will be envious today." See how many evils you are allowing yourself! But if it is good for you to pay attention tomorrow, how much better it would be to do so today. You may be able to achieve the same tomorrow as well, without putting it off again for the day after.

Think about this

So, is it possible to be altogether faultless? No, that is impracticable; but it is possible to strive continuously not to commit faults. Discourses IV.12.19. Epictetus [GC/RH]

CHAPTER 13

Freedom from Divulging Confidences

Key ideas of this discourse

1. *If someone confides in you, you don't have to confide back.*

2. *You confide in someone only if that person is trustworthy.*

3. *As a rule, confidences require good faith and judgments that go with it.*

If someone confides in you, you don't have to confide back

When someone gives you the impression that they have talked frankly about their personal lives, we somehow feel compelled to share our own secrets with them. We suppose that we are being frank. In the first place, it seems unfair to receive our neighbour's confidences without sharing your own with them. Next, we think that others wouldn't think we are frank, if we keep quiet about our personal affairs. Indeed, people often say, "Now that I've told you all about my affairs. Aren't you willing to tell me anything about yours? Why?" We also think that we can safely trust someone who has trusted us with their secrets. We feel that the other person would never reveal our secrets for fear we would reveal theirs.

It is in this way that soldiers at Rome catch out people who are not careful. A soldier in civilian clothes sits down beside you and begins to speak ill of Caesar. You feel you received from him a guarantee of good faith because he was the one who began the abuse. So, you tell him what you think and the next thing you know, you are restrained and put in prison.

We experience something similar in our daily life. Even though this person has safely confided his secrets to me, for my part, I won't trust anyone who comes along. No, I listen, and keep silent (if I am that kind of person) but he goes out and tells everybody. When I learn what has happened, I tell his secrets to everyone, out of a desire for revenge. So, I defame him, and he defames me.

However, if I remember that one person cannot harm another, and that one is helped or harmed by one's own actions, I achieve at least this much: I don't act in the same way as the other person does. I get into trouble because of my own foolish actions.

"Yes, but isn't it unfair to listen to your neighbour's secrets and give him no share of your own in return?"

"Man, you didn't invite his confidence, did you? Did the other person tell you about his affairs on condition that you tell him yours? If he is a chatterbox and takes anyone he meets as a friend, do you also want to be like him? If he did well to trust you with his confidences, but if it won't be good for you to trust him in return, do you want to be so rash to do so?"

It is as though I have a water-tight barrel and you have one with a hole in it. You come and deposit your wine with me, for me to store in my jar. You then complain that I don't deposit my wine with you. Of course, not! Your barrel has a hole in it. How are they equal? You deposited your property to a trustworthy man, a man of honour; a man who believes that only his own actions, not externals, can bring him harm or help. Do you want me to make a deposit with you, a man who has dishonoured his own faculty of choice? To someone who wants to get some money, some office, or some public recognition, even if it means murdering his own children, as Medea did? Where's the equality in that?

You confide in someone only if that person is trustworthy

But show me that you are trustworthy, respectful, and dependable; show me that your judgments are those of a friend; show me that your vessel is not leaky. Then you'll see that, instead of waiting for you to confide in me, I will

confide in you first. Who doesn't want to use a good vessel? Who despises a friendly and faithful adviser? Who
doesn't gladly welcome someone to share the burden of
his troubles and make them lighter?

"Yes, I trust you, but you don't trust me."

"First of all, you don't trust me either. You're simply
a babbler, that's why you can't keep anything to yourself."

If you really trust me, then confide only in me. Instead, whenever you see someone who is at leisure, you
sit by his side and say, "Brother, there's no one who is
kindlier disposed or dearer to me than you. I invite you
to listen to my affairs." And you do this with people
whom you not have known even for a short while. Even
if you trust me, it is clearly because you trust me as a
faithful and honourable person and not because I have
told you my affairs. Allow me, then, to have the same
thought about you. Show me that, if a person tells someone about his own affairs, it follows that the person is
faithful and honourable. If this was the case, I would go
around telling everyone about my affairs.

But that's not the case. To be faithful and honourable,
one needs to have judgments that are not ordinary. If you
see someone, then, who is concerned about things outside their area of choice, making his own choice second-
ary to them, you will find thousands of people
constraining and obstructing him. You don't need the
pitch or the wheel [ancient methods of torture] to make
him say what he knows. Even the slightest nod from a
pretty girl, if it so happens, is enough to shake him. As

will a friendly gesture from someone at Caesar's court, a desire for public office, an inheritance, and thirty thousand things of that sort.

So, remember, as a rule, confidences require good faith and judgments that go with it. Where, these days, can you find them easily? Let someone show me someone who is of such a good way that he can say, "I care only for what is my own, what is not subject to obstruction, and what is by nature free. This is what's truly good and I have this. Let all else happen as God wishes. It makes no difference to me.'

Think about this

One person does not harm another, but it is a man's own actions which both harm and help him. Discourses IV.13.8. Epictetus [WO]

Who Was Arrian?

Arrian of Nicomedia

Flavius Arrianus or Arrian of Nicomedia (c. 86 – c.146 CE), the scribe of Epictetus' Discourses, was a distinguished Greek historian, military commander, public official, and philosopher. He was a student of Epictetus, presumably in his late teens, and took extensive notes of Epictetus' discourses. They were presumed to be dialogues between Epictetus and his pupils and other visitors and not notes of class room lectures. These discourses were collected in eight notebooks, only four of them survive.

He was distinguished in many fields, For example, his *Anabasis of Alexander* is considered the best source companion of Alexander the Great. Among his other works is also a history of India.

The authenticity of Discourses

Epictetus did not directly author Discourses or Enchiridion or any of the other things attributed to him. It was his illustrious student who kept notes of Epictetus Discourses, presumably for personal use.

Given that these were the notes of a young student, how much can we rely on them? How authentic a record are they of Epictetus' teachings?

Many scholars considered the question and generally believe that Arrian's Discourses to be a faithful recording of the teacher. There are many reasons for this:

- Arrian was intellectually distinguished.
- His other books read differently. They were written in a more formal Greek rather than in the colloquial Greek (Koine Greek) used in *Discourses*.
- *Discourses* was published while Epictetus was still alive. So if it was a misinterpretation of Epictetus teachings, either he or his followers would have challenged it. No such challenge appears to be on record.
- The discourses are highly repetitive. We would assume that if the discourses were made up, they would be more carefully crafted, especially by someone of Arrain's stature.
- The same tone of Epictetus' voice is evident in all discourses.

So it is reasonable for us to assume that Arrian's *Discourses* is an authentic (or near-authentic) record of the master's teachings.

The publication of Discourses

It appears that these books of Epictetus' Discourses were published without Arrian's knowledge or consent, as he explains in his letter to the Roman politician and supporter of Cicero, Lucius Gellius (presumably a friend). Arrian seemed to have been quite surprised by the publication of his personal notes, as his letter shows.

Arrian's Letter to Lucius Gellius

Greetings.

I neither composed the Discourses of Epictetus in such a manner as things of this nature are commonly composed, nor did I myself produce them to public view, any more than I composed them. But whatever sentiments I heard from his own mouth, the very same I endeavoured to set down in the very same words, so far as possible, and to preserve as memorials for my own use, of his manner of thinking, and freedom of speech.

These Discourses are such as one person would naturally deliver from his own thoughts, extempore, to another; not such as he would prepare to be read by numbers afterwards. Yet, notwithstanding this, I cannot tell how, without either my consent or knowledge, they have fallen into the hands of the public. But it is of little consequence to me, if I do not appear an able writer, and of none to Epictetus, if any one treats his Discourses with contempt; since it was very evident, even when he uttered them, that he aimed at nothing more than to excite his hearers to virtue. If they produce that one effect, they have in them what, I think, philosophical discourses ought to have. And should they fail of it, let the readers however be assured, that when Epictetus himself pronounced them, his audience could not help being affected in the very manner he intended they should. If by themselves they have less efficacy, perhaps it is my fault, or perhaps it is unavoidable.

Farewell.

What About the Four Lost Books?

The Four Lost Books

It is generally believed that Arrian compiled Discourses in eight volumes, only four of which survive. Given that we have lost about half of all Arrian's compilations, one naturally wonders if we have lost something substantial with regard to Epictetus' thinking. No one can provide a definitive answer to that question, of course.

However, when one looks at the structure of the Discourses, it becomes clear that, after the first few discourses, very few new ideas are introduced. Many discourses are an expansion of the earlier discourses, or they repeat the same ideas in different words, often using different examples. Occasionally, some later discourses repeat an earlier idea using the same words and examples. The redundancy is so pronounced that a modern translator (Robert Dobbin) of Discourses did not even care to translate two-thirds of books III and IV (18 out of 26 and 8 out of 13)

Again, in Enchiridion (which is essentially a summary of the essence of Epictetus' teachings) we don't find any new ideas not found in the first four books.

So while it is possible that we might have missed some of the rhetorical flourishes of Epictetus, it seems unlikely that the four lost books contained any new ideas not covered in the books that survived.

APPENDIX 3

A Note on
This Version of Discourses

How is this plain English version different?

The first four volumes in this series (Stoic Foundations, Stoic Choices, Stoic Training, and Stoic) are a plain English version of Epictetus' Discourses as transcribed by Arrian.

This is not a reinterpretation of Epictetus, but a re-expression so the language and the idiom follow modern English, expressed in a simple and straightforward way. The main purpose of this rendering is to make the works of Epictetus easily accessible to a modern reader. Here is how this rendering compares with literal translations:

Chapter titles

The chapter titles in the original were often either cryptic or non-descriptive of the content of the discourse, such as 'To Naso,' or 'Of Providence.' I changed them to make it descriptive of the content of the discourse and the main theme of each book.

Chapter subheadings

The original *Discourses* had no chapter subheads. The translations used a numbering system which served no purpose (except as a point of reference) and was intrusive. I eliminated the numbering system and added subheads to make it easier to read and locate a passage of interest.

Commentary

Throughout these books, I have added commentary to provide clarity to the content. Other authors generally have them as endnotes, but I have chosen to include it in the text itself because I felt that it makes less work for the reader. Commentaries are clearly set apart from the main text itself by square brackets and, in some cases, italicized font.

Occasional minor changes

To make it relevant to the modern reader, I have occasionally made minor changes. For example, if there was a reference to an obscure wrestler, I might have omitted the reference to the name of the wrestler but just referred that person as 'a wrestler.' If there was a reference to a 'bath house,' I might have changed it to a 'swimming pool.' But in all cases I have retained intended meaning.

Occasional shortening of a repetitive dialogue

Because *Discourses* is an unedited transcript of Epictetus' conversations, sometimes a lengthy dialogue could contain repetition which does not add to the content. Occasionally, when it is highly repetitious, I have shortened it slightly.

Minor changes in sentence sequence

Because *Discourses* are transcripts of dialogues, the sentence sequences are not what it would be in a written text. In a few instances, where I felt rearranging a few sentences would improve clarity, I have done so.

Choosing the simplest interpretation

Sometimes the same word is translated differently by different scholars. For example, the same word is translated as 'bad' by some and as 'evil' by others; the same phrase is translated as 'moral choice,' 'sphere of choice,' or 'judgment' by different translators. In cases where there are different interpretations, I have chosen to accept the interpretations that are easiest to understand as well as most widely acceptable.

Choosing a simplified, modern format

Discourses, is essentially a series of conversations and lectures by Epictetus. He often uses the Socratic dialogue technique to clarify issues raised by students and visitors. Sometimes, the discourses are probably monologues structured as dialogues. However, in most translations, they are not formatted as conversations, so the immediacy of the question and answer is muted. So, wherever possible, I have formatted them as conversations (which most of them actually were), until they become long monologues. I believe that this change in formatting not only makes the book easier to read but also brings forth the immediacy of the issues raised.

The gender issue

Epictetus' students were (almost?) exclusively male. Again, until a few years ago, unspecified masculine pronouns stood for both genders. So, it is safe to assume that when Epictetus says 'a man,' he means 'a person,' and when he says 'he,' Epictetus means either 'she' or 'he.' Stoic teachings are equally applicable to members of both genders. But in modern usage, the exclusive use of masculine pronouns would be considered sexist.

Consequently I have alternated between masculine and feminine pronouns throughout the text. Even more commonly, I have changed it to the second person singular (For example, instead of 'A man cannot ...,' 'You cannot.)

Sources consulted

In preparing these five books, my main concern was to be as faithful to the teachings of Epictetus as possible. I am no scholar of ancient Greek and to make sure that I don't inadvertently distort Epictetus' words, I consulted several translations starting with the first English translation by Elizabeth Carter (revised editions) and ending with the latest translation by Robin Hard (2014). The translations I consulted included the following:

- Higginson, Thomas Wentworth (1865). *The Complete Works of Epictetus*. Based on Elizabeth Carter's Translation.
- Long, George (1877) *Discourses of Epictetus*. Delphi edition.
- Oldfather, William A (1928) *Epictetus: Volumes I and II*. Loeb Edition.
- Hard, Robin, Christopher Gill, ed. (1995) *The Discourses, The Handbook, Fragments*. Everyman (J.M. Dent). Elizabeth Carter's translation updated.
- Hard, Robin (2014) *Discourses, Fragments, Handbook*. Oxford World Classics. (The only compete translation of *Discourses* since 1920, as of 2017.)
- Dobbin, Robert (2008 *Discourses and Selected Writings*. Penguin. (Based on the Greek text prepared by J. Souhile of Paris)

Resolving contradictions

The translations weren't consistent. Sometimes the same passages were translated differently by different translators. Most of these differences were minor and they weren't meaningful enough to warrant an investigation. However, there were a couple of passages which were translated so differently, that I consulted other experts on Stoicism such as Massimo Pigliucci and Christopher

Gill to resolve the issues. Chis Gill was particularly helpful in resolving a contradiction involved in a crucial passage.

Although it is not the purpose of this rendering to be an authoritative source, I have done as much as I can to make it as authoritative as possible, given that this is not a literal translation of the original. Whenever plain English would not allow me to be close to the original in structure, I tried to make sure it is close to the original in meaning and spirit. It is my belief that, for most of us who are not scholars, minor losses in accuracy is a small price to pay to gain a better appreciation of Epictetus and what he was trying to teach us.

Concordance of
Discourses Titles

The discourse titles

As I mentioned in Appendix 3, I have changed the titles to make them more descriptive of the content. Here I provide a list of the original titles followed by the titles used in this series.

If you would like to cross-reference any of the discourses with any other version, you can use this concordance tables to identify the discourse in other versions.

The original titles are given first, followed by the title used in this series.

Concordance

Book 1. Stoic Foundations

I.: OF THE THINGS WHICH ARE, AND THE THINGS WHICH ARE NOT IN OUR OWN POWER.

Understand What is in Your Power

II.: IN WHAT MANNER, UPON EVERY OCCASION, TO PRESERVE OUR CHARACTER.

Act Your Best. You Can Endure Anything.

III.: HOW, FROM THE DOCTRINE THAT GOD IS THE FATHER OF MANKIND, WE MAY PROCEED TO ITS CONSEQUENCES.

Don't Become a Treacherous Animal

IV: OF PROGRESS.

How to Know you are Making Progress

V.: CONCERNING THE ACADEMICS.†

Beware of Rigid Thinking

VI.: OF PROVIDENCE.

Don't Complain. You Have no Reason to

VII.: OF THE USE OF THE FORMS OF RIGHT REASONING.

Deal with Arguments in a Logical Way

VIII.: THAT LOGICAL SUBTLETIES ARE NOT SAFE TO THE UNINSTRUCTED.

Distinguish the Important from the Incidental

IX.: HOW FROM THE DOCTRINE OF OUR RELATIONSHIP TO GOD, WE ARE TO DEDUCE ITS CONSEQUENCES.

Behave Like you are Related to god

X.: CONCERNING THOSE WHO SEEK PREFERMENT AT ROME.

Book 2. Stoic Choices

Book 3. Stoic Training

Book 4. Stoic Freedom.

I.: OF FREEDOM.

How to Achieve Freedom

II.: OF COMPLAISANCE.

Be Committed to Your Choice

III.: WHAT THINGS ARE TO BE EXCHANGED FOR OTHERS.

Guard Your Freedom

IV.: CONCERNING THOSE WHO EARNESTLY DESIRE A LIFE OF REPOSE.

Act on What You Learned

V.: CONCERNING THE QUARRELSOME AND FEROCIOUS.

Freedom from Conflicts

VI.: CONCERNING THOSE WHO ARE ANNOYED AT BEING PITIED.

Freedom from the Opinion of Others

VII.: OF FEARLESSNESS.

Freedom from Fear

VIII.: CONCERNING SUCH AS HASTILY ASSUME THE PHILOSOPHIC DRESS.

Freedom from Hasty Judgments

IX.: CONCERNING A PERSON WHO HAD GROWN IMMODEST.

Freedom from Following the Wrong Course

X.: WHAT THINGS WE ARE TO DESPISE, AND WHAT CHIEFLY TO VALUE.

Freedom from Anxieties

XI.: OF PURITY.

Freedom from Uncleanliness

XII.: OF TAKING PAINS.

Freedom from Mind Wandering

XIII.: CONCERNING SUCH AS ARE TOO COMMUNICA-
TIVE.

Freedom from Divulging Confidences

Free Online Resources

Free resources

At least a couple of earlier translations are available free online. These translations contain all four books of Discourses

Thomas Wentworth Higgins (based on Elizabeth Carter's translation) Download for free from:
http://oll.libertyfund.org/titles/epictetus-the-works-of-epictetus-consisting-of-his-discourses-in-four-books#lf0755_label_195

A Selection from the Discourses of Epictetus with the Enchiridion. Download from Amazon.
https://www.amazon.com/Selection-Discourses-Epictetus-Encheiridion-ebook/dp/B008401Z3E/ref=sr_1_1?s=digital-text&ie=UTF8&qid=1511136743&sr=1-1&keywords=epictetus+discourses

In addition, you may also be download older translations from Amazon for a very small amount (such as $1)

ABOUT THE AUTHOR

Dr Chuck Chakrapani. He has been a long-term, but embarrassingly inconsistent, practitioner of Stoicism. He is the president of Leger Analytics, Chief Knowledge Officer of The Blackstone Group in Chicago and a Distinguished Visiting Professor at Ryerson University.

Chuck has written books on several subjects over the years which include research methods, statistics, and investment strategies. His personal website is Chuck-Chakrapani.com

His books on Stoicism include *Unshakable Freedom*, *A Fortunate Storm* and *The Good Life Handbook* (a rendering of Epictetus' Enchiridion.)

ALSO BY THE AUTHOR

Stoic Foundations

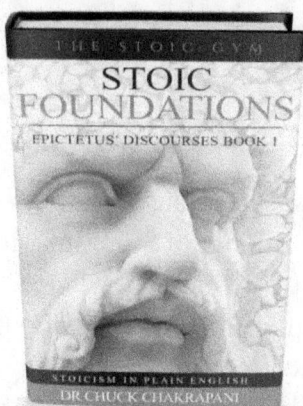

Stoic Foundations is the plain English version of Discourses Book 1 by the eminent Stoic philosopher Epictetus.

It revolves around 10 themes which are also repeated in other places throughout Discourses. These are:

- Concern yourself with only what is in your power
- Be content to let things happen as they do
- Your thinking, not the externals, drives your behaviour
- Do not place value on external things
- Don't give in to your anger or animal instincts
- You can handle anything; always act your best
  Learn to think properly and logically
- Practice, not knowledge, results in progress
- Only you can make you happy

Available from your favourite online bookstore.

Stoic Choices

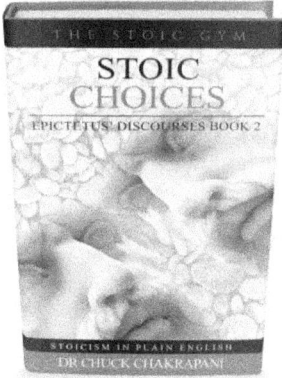

Stoic Choices is the plain English version of Discourses Book 2 by the eminent Stoic philosopher Epictetus.

It revolves around 10 themes which are also repeated in other places throughout Discourses. Here are some of the choices discussed in this book:

- What should you act upon: External things or internal things?
- When should you choose to be confident and when to be cautious in making decisions?
- What should you protect: Your inherent qualities or qualities that are not inherent to you?
- Is there a choice between knowledge and action?
- Is there a choice between knowledge and anxiety?
- Should you study logic? Why?
- Choose to be faithful.
- Choose habits that fight impressions.
- Show yourself to be worthy.
- Choose to be skilful.

Available from your favourite online bookstore

Stoic Training

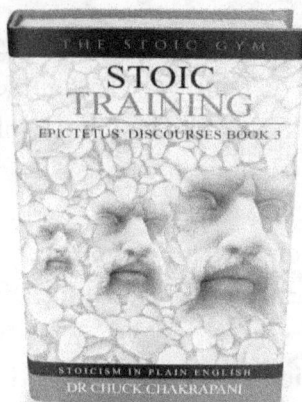

This is the third book of *Discourses* of Epictetus in plain English. Stoics did not believe in just theoretical knowledge but held that it is critical we practice what we learned. Here are the basic themes of Stoic training explored by Epictetus here:

- Stoic training aims to make you excellent as a human being.
- Stoic training consists of three disciplines: desire, action and assent.
- Stoic training consists only of dealing with one's choices.
- Train you mind to want whatever actually happens.
- Stoic training means to prepare ourselves for the challenges to come.
- Ascetic training is unnecessary unless it serves some purpose.
- Train to see things as they are without adding your judgements to them.
- Your judgements are the sole cause of your distress, because nothing outside of you can harm you.
- Don't imitate others without understanding the basis of their actions.]
- Train to be at home wherever you are. Things are impermanent.
- Your goal is happiness and good fortune.

Coming Soon - Stoic Inspirations

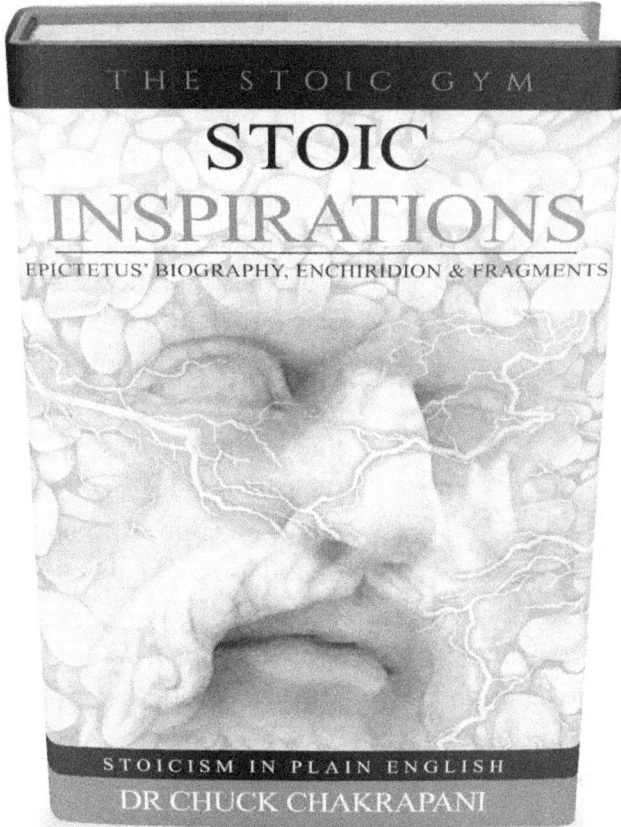

Stoic Inspirations combines the Enchiridion (Epictetus'
pupil Arrian's notebook summarizing his teachings) and
the remaining fragments of the lost Discourses books. It
completes the Stoicism in Plain English series on Epictetus from The Stoic Gym.

A Fortunate Storm

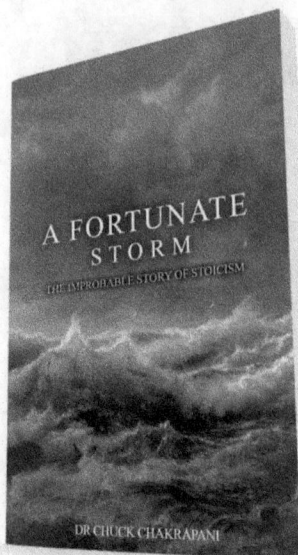

Unshakable Freedom is based on Stoic teachings.

But how did Stoicism come about?

Three unconnected events – a shipwreck in Piraeus, a play in Thebes, and the banishment of a rebel in Turkey – connected three unrelated individuals to give birth to a philosophy. It was to endure two thousand years and offer hope and comfort to hundreds of thousands of people along the way.

The Fortunate Storm is the improbable story of how Stoicism came about. You can get a FREE COPY of the e-version of this book at the link below:

http://www.TheStoicGym.com/fortunatestormfree

The Good Life Handbook

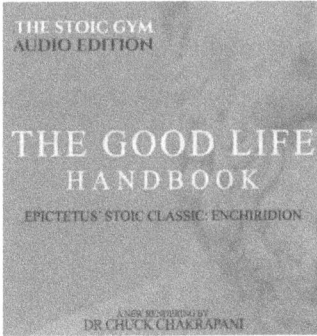

Available in Print, digital, and audio editions.

The Good Life Handbook is a rendering of Enchiridion in plain English. It is a concise summary of the teachings of Epictetus, as transcribed and later summarized by his student Flavius Arrian.

The Handbook is a guide to the good life. It answers the question, "How can we be good and live free and happy, no matter what else is happening around us?"

Ancient Stoics lived in a time of turmoil under difficult conditions. So, the solutions they found to living free was tested under very stringent conditions. For example, the author of this Handbook was a lame slave who made himself free and happy later in life by following the principles set out in this book.

Now The Stoic Gym offers *The Good Life Handbook* by Dr Chuck Chakrapani to interested readers free (Kindle and other online versions).

Please get your copy in your favourite online bookstore.

Unshakable Freedom

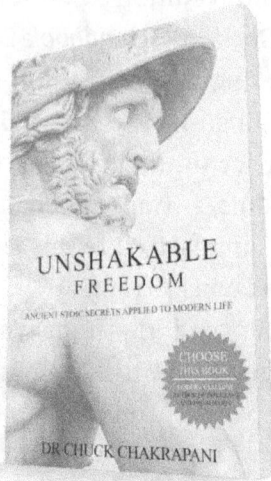

How can we achieve total personal freedom when we have so many obligations and so many demands on our time? Is personal freedom even possible?

Yes, it is possible, said the Stoics and gave us a blue print for freedom. The teachings were lost but have been rediscovered in recent times and form the basis of modern cognitive therapy.

In his new book, *Unshakable Freedom*, Dr Chuck Chakrapani outlines the Stoic secrets for achieving total freedom, no matter who you are and what obstacles you face in life.

Using modern examples, Chuck explores how anyone can achieve personal freedom by practicing a few mind-training techniques

www.ingramcontent.com/pod-product-compliance
Lightning Source LLC
LaVergne TN
LVHW021452080426
835509LV00018B/2258